cooking with
CHEESE

Better Homes and Gardens

cooking with

CHEESE

BETTER HOMES AND GARDENS BOOKS
NEW YORK   DES MOINES

CONTENTS

Cheese Guide. 6
Magnificent Main Dishes. 12
Dips, Spreads, and Tidbits. 40
Breads and Sandwiches. 48
Salads and Vegetables. 60
Soups and Sauces. 70
Desserts. 76
Index. 89

On our cover, Golden Velvet Rabbit is ladled over bacon waffle triangles. Flecks of pimiento spike complementary flavors of Muenster and American cheese.

Preview two dazzling cheese recipes! Swiss Luncheon Special features Swiss cheese baked with hard-cooked eggs in creamy sauce. Thin noodles are tossed with Romano cheese and cream cheese sauce in Noodles Romano.

Our checked seal assures you that every recipe in Cooking with Cheese is tested and endorsed by the Better Homes and Gardens Test Kitchen. Each dish must measure up to high standards of family appeal, practicality, and deliciousness!

Cheese guide

Camembert (kam′-em-bear). Savor the creamy yellow, almost liquid interior, piquant flavor! And do eat the thin grayish crust! Serve at room temperature as appetizer or dessert.

Cream. This versatile cheese stars in appetizers, salads, main dishes, and desserts. You'll find foil-wrapped pieces and jars of plain cheese or cheese with seasonings such as chives or pimiento added. Use the whipped form for dips.

Gourmandise (goor-mahn-deez′). A soft, creamy French cheese spread subtly flavored with kirsch, a cherry brandy. Serve as appetizer or dessert.

Club. This blend of natural cheeses, frequently Cheddar or Swiss, may have condiments, wine, or flavorings, such as smoke, added. An appetizer or dessert cheese, it spreads well.

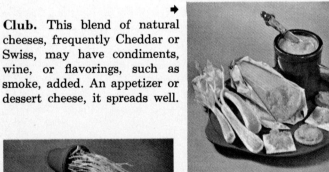

Cottage. Also known as pot cheese or schmierkase, it comes in large or small curd, plain or creamed, and with fruits, chives, or vegetables added.

Liederkranz(lee′-dir-krahnz). Made exclusively in the U.S., this cheese is similar to Limburger but less pungent. The robust flavor makes it an ideal appetizer or dessert. Incidentally, the name means "wealth of songs."

Limburger. Cheese-lovers relish the pungent flavor of this appetizer cheese, available in pieces or as a spread. First made in Belgium, it is now made in the U. S. also. Cheese-makers say it's among the most delicate to produce.

Ricotta (ri-kah'-tuh). This smooth, creamy cheese is similar to cottage cheese. A basic ingredient in lasagne, it is used in many other Italian dishes. The sweet nutlike flavor complements appetizers and dessert dishes as well.

Bel Paese (bel-pah-ay'-ze). The mild flavor and soft texture of this Italian appetizer or dessert cheese is protected by individual wooden boxes.

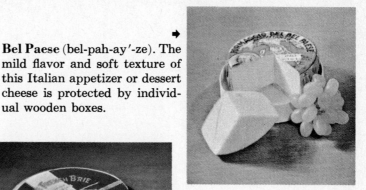

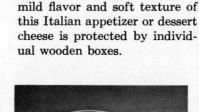

Neufchatel (new-sha-tell'). Although lower in fat content this cheese is a cream cheese "twin." It's available in pieces and a variety of spreads.

Brick. This mild to sharp cheese originated in America and was brick-shaped and sized (now also sold sliced). Serve as an appetizer or dessert.

Brie (bree). Originally French, now made in U.S., the creamy yellow interior is encased by thin edible crust. The mild to pungent flavor complements appetizers, desserts.

Blue. On imported brands the spelling is "bleu." The name comes from veins of friendly mold which give cheese tangy, peppy flavor. Delicious as appetizer, dessert, or in salad.

Gruyere (gree-air′). This nutty-flavored process cheese melts easily for fondue, makes ideal dessert with fruit and crackers. Natural form is also available.

Port du Salut (por-du-Sa-lu′). French Trappist monks make this cheese which is similar to Canadian Oka, but has a more pronounced flavor. It's great with apple pie as well as other desserts and appetizers. A Danish variety is also shown.

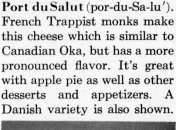

Monterey Jack. A great West Coast favorite from California sometimes called "Jack" cheese. Its mild flavor and creamy texture make it especially good in appetizer or main dish recipes.

Roquefort (rok-for′). The original blue-veined cheese comes from French caves and is made from sheep's milk. Blue, Gorgonzola, and Stilton are related.

Mozzarella, Scamorze (mah-tsa-rel′-la, ska-mort′-za). Both of these are favorite cheeses for use in pizza. Mozzarella comes sliced or shredded while Scamorze comes in small rolls.

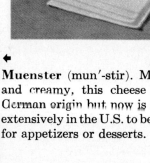

Muenster (mun′-stir). Mellow and creamy, this cheese is of German origin but now is made extensively in the U.S. to be used for appetizers or desserts.

Tilsit (till′-sit). Mild and mellow in flavor with a rather open texture, this Danish cheese comes plain or studded with caraway, as shown here. Chunks are cut from large rectangular loaves to be served for appetizer or dessert.

Blarney. Sold in wedge cuts, the bright red coating and the interior color of this Irish cheese remind you of Edam, and the small "eyes" remind you of Swiss. The flavor is wonderful whether it be for appetizer, main dish, or dessert.

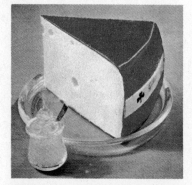

Cheddar. Undoubtedly the most popular cheese in U.S., it has a mild, medium, or sharp flavor, depending on age. First made in Cheddar, England.

Fontina (fon-tee′-na). Italian table cheese with scattered "eyes." Has a creamy to light yellow color and mellow flavor, is firm-textured and easy to slice for appetizers or desserts.

Gjetost (yea′-toast). Shaved thin on crackers, this Norwegian goat's-milk cheese, often called the "brown sugar" cheese, is a real appetizer or dessert treat.

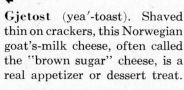

Double Gloucester (glah′-stir). Wedges of this centuries-old English favorite are cut from a large "millstone." It's golden in color and mellow in flavor, used for appetizers or desserts.

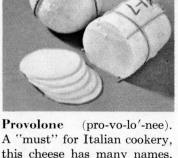

Provolone (pro-vo-lo′-nee). A "must" for Italian cookery, this cheese has many names, depending on size and shape— Provolette, Provoloncini, or Salami Provolone. It also comes sliced. All have a smoked, sharp flavor.

Edam and Gouda (ee′-dum, goo′-da). Both mildly flavored, the "cannon balls" in picture are Edams. The flattened rounds, Gouda and Baby Gouda, are higher in fat.

Riksost (rik′-soast). "Farmer's cheese" from Sweden comes in rounds of 2 pounds. Cut in half, then in semicircles for appetizer or dessert.

Process American Cheese. A blend of fresh and aged natural cheeses is pasteurized to prevent further ripening. The resulting smooth cheese has excellent cooking qualities. It may have pimiento, meat, or smoke flavor added.

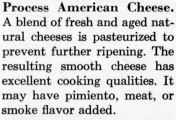

Sapsago (sap′-say-go). The green cheese that the moon is made from owes its color and flavor to cloverlike plant. Used for appetizer, main dish.

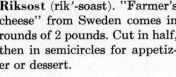
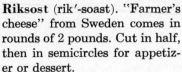

Process Cheese Foods. Milk or whey solids are added to process cheese. Flavoring agents may also be added.

Swiss. Sweet nutty flavor is appropriate throughout the meal. This distinctive "eyed" cheese originated in Switzerland, also made in U.S.

Natural Cheese. This includes all cheeses made directly from milk solids which are separated from milk by use of rennet and/ or bacterial culture.

Parmesan (pahr-ma-zahn′) **Romano** (ro-mah′-no). Famous grating cheeses, they are as basic as tomatoes to Italian main dishes; also, appetizers.

Process Cheese Spreads. Like cheese foods, except they have a higher moisture content and lower milk fat content. Stabilizer prevents separation. Spread easily at room temperature; melt quickly in cooking. Available plain or flavored.

Give cheese loving care

STORAGE TIPS

Refrigerate natural cheese in the original wrapper. Cover cut surfaces tightly with foil or clear plastic wrap. Dip the cut surfaces of large pieces of cheese in hot paraffin before refrigerating. Properly stored, natural cheeses will keep for several weeks.

Store aromatic or strong flavored cheeses, such as Limburger, refrigerated in a tightly covered jar. Refrigerate cottage cheese, cream cheese, and Neufchatel immediately as they are highly perishable. Use soon after purchase.

Keep process cheeses at room temperature before they are opened, if desired. Store tightly wrapped in the refrigerator after opening.

Freezing cheese is not generally recommended. However, Brick, Cheddar, Edam, Gouda, Muenster, Port du Salut, Swiss, Provolone, Mozzarella, and Camembert may be frozen satisfactorily with slightly altered texture.

Freeze 1 pound or less in pieces not over 1 inch thick. Package tightly in moisture vapor-proof freezer wrapping and freeze at 0° or below. Thaw in the refrigerator and use as soon as possible. It will keep several months.

COOKING AND SERVING HINTS

The mold which may develop on cheese is not harmful. Scrape mold off surface before using. Grate ends or hard pieces of cheese and store in tightly covered jar. Use for garnish.

When cooking cheese, use low heat and do not overcook. High temperatures and prolonged cooking will toughen the cheese. As a result, the product will be stringy and curdled. Remember, when cheese is melted, it is cooked.

For peak flavor, let all cheeses (except cottage cheese or cream cheese) stand at room temperature for 30 minutes before serving.

The complement of wines

The marriage of wine and cheese has become an age-old legend. As the story is retold, various customs change. Such adaptations enable people around the world to enjoy wine and cheese according to local traditions. Thus, a perfect partnership is perpetuated.

Appetizer wines are offered before a meal to stimulate the appetite. Dry or cocktail Sherry and dry Vermouth are served chilled with sharp cheese and crackers, well-seasoned cheese dips, or cheese canapes. Appetizer wines may be "fortified" with brandy or other spirits.

Dry red table wines are considered good companions for cheese entrees. The more robust Burgundy accompanies cheese main dishes made from sharp, nippy cheese. Claret is a good choice for mild cheese casseroles and fondue. The Italian special, Chianti, complements spaghetti and pizza. Serve these wines at cool room temperature (about 60°). Draw the cork half an hour before serving to allow the wine to "breathe" and to develop bouquet.

Rose wine, another red wine, pleases most palates and goes with almost all foods as well. This versatile wine enjoys grand popularity in America where it is served chilled throughout the meal.

White table wines are pleasant accompaniments for some cheese dishes. Dry white wines such as Sauterne, Chablis, and Rhine may be served chilled with light cheese dishes. This might include egg and cheese dishes, macaroni and cheese, or rice and cheese.

Dessert wines are usually sweeter and may be fortified with other spirits. Port and Cream Sherry are served at room temperature, with or after dessert. They're especially good with a tray of assorted cheese and fruit.

Sparkling wines such as Champagne or Sparkling Rose accompany special occasion foods throughout the meal. Sparkling Burgundy is especially good with cheese main dishes. These festive wines should be stored flat on their side and served chilled.

MAGNIFICENT MAIN DISHES

Sunshine casseroles abound
with rich melted cheese.

Cheese and eggs: royal fare
for family and friends alike.

South of the border specialties
bring a touch of Mexico.

Prize pizza provides a popular
way to please the palate.

Saucy specials feature Swiss
fondue and creamy rabbits.

Main dishes starring meat and
cheese offer exciting duos.

Chicken and turkey with cheese
assures perfect partners.

Sea food favorites include flavorful fish and cheese.

Parmesan Omelet, a cloud-like puff
cloaked in golden Cheddar sauce. Each
forkful will melt in your mouth.

Sunshine casseroles

HAMBURGER-CHEESE DELIGHT

1 pound ground beef
1 medium onion, chopped
2 8-ounce cans tomato sauce
1 teaspoon salt
1 teaspoon sugar
¼ teaspoon *each* garlic salt and pepper
4 cups medium noodles
1 cup cream-style cottage cheese
1 8-ounce package cream cheese,
　softened
¼ cup dairy sour cream
⅓ cup sliced green onions
¼ cup chopped green pepper
¼ cup grated Parmesan cheese

Cook beef and onion till brown. Stir in next 5 ingredients. Remove from heat. Cook noodles using package directions; drain. Meanwhile, combine next 5 ingredients. Spread *half* the noodles in 11x7x1½-inch baking dish. Moisten with some of the hamburger sauce. Cover with cheese mixture. Top with remaining noodles, then hamburger sauce. Sprinkle with Parmesan. Bake at 350° for 30 minutes. Serves 8 to 10.

HUNGARIAN NOODLE BAKE

3 cups fine noodles
1 clove garlic, minced
¼ cup finely chopped onion
1 tablespoon butter or margarine
1½ cups cream-style cottage cheese
1 cup dairy sour cream
1 teaspoon Worcestershire sauce
Dash bottled hot pepper sauce
2 teaspoons poppy seed
½ teaspoon salt
Dash pepper

Cook noodles in boiling salted water till tender; drain. Meanwhile, cook garlic and onion in butter till tender but not brown. Combine noodles and onion mixture with remaining ingredients. Bake in a greased 10x6x1½-inch baking dish at 350° for 25 minutes. Serve with grated Parmesan cheese. Serves 6.

NOODLES ROMANO

¼ cup soft butter or margarine
2 tablespoons parsley flakes
1 teaspoon crushed basil
1 8-ounce package cream cheese,
　softened
Dash pepper
⅔ cup boiling water
. . .
1 8-ounce package fettucini, thin
　noodles, or spaghetti
1 clove garlic, minced
¼ cup butter or margarine
¾ cup shredded or grated Romano or
　Parmesan cheese

Combine the soft butter, parsley flakes, and basil; blend in cream cheese and pepper; stir in boiling water; blend well. Keep warm.
Cook noodles in large amount boiling salted water till just tender; drain. Cook garlic in the ¼ cup butter 1 to 2 minutes; pour over noodles; toss lightly and quickly to coat well. Sprinkle with ½ *cup* of the cheese; toss again. Pile noodles on warm serving platter; spoon the warm cream cheese sauce over; sprinkle with remaining ¼ cup cheese. Toss slightly to blend. Garnish with parsley. Makes 6 servings.

FRANKS FLORENTINE

1 10-ounce package frozen chopped
　spinach, cooked and drained
1½ cups cooked rice
1 11-ounce can condensed Cheddar
　cheese soup
2 tablespoons minced onion
¼ cup milk
½ pound (4 to 5) frankfurters, halved
　crosswise

Spread spinach in bottom of 10x6x1½-inch baking dish. Combine rice, soup, onion, and milk; spoon over spinach. Score halved franks with an X-shape cut; arrange on casserole, pressing into rice. Bake in moderate oven (375°) for 20 to 25 minutes. Makes 4 servings.

CHEESE-RICE SQUARES

Cheese mingles with rice; parsley adds the zip—

**3 cups cooked rice
4 ounces sharp process American
   cheese, shredded (1 cup)
½ cup snipped parsley
¼ cup minced onion
1 teaspoon salt
½ teaspoon monosodium glutamate
    . . .
3 beaten eggs
1½ cups milk
1 teaspoon Worcestershire sauce**

Mix rice, cheese, parsley, onion, and seasonings. Combine eggs, milk, and Worcestershire; add to rice mixture and mix thoroughly. Pour into greased 10x6x1½-inch baking dish. Bake in slow oven (325°) for 40 to 45 minutes or just till set. Cut in squares; top with your favorite creamed chicken or tuna. Serves 6 to 8.

CORNED BEEF SUPPER SPECIAL

One delicious cheesey dish combines both meat and vegetables—perfect for a hurry-up supper—

**1 10½-ounce can condensed cream of
   chicken soup
4 ounces sharp process American
   cheese, shredded (1 cup)
¼ teaspoon salt
    . . .
2 1-pound cans (4 cups) tiny whole
   potatoes, drained
2 1-pound cans (4 cups) small whole
   onions, drained
1 3-ounce can broiled sliced
   mushrooms, drained (½ cup)
½ cup chopped green pepper
    . . .
1 12-ounce can corned beef, chilled
1 cup buttered soft bread crumbs or
   corn flake crumbs**

Combine soup, cheese, and salt. Add potatoes, onions, mushrooms, and green pepper. Pour into greased 8x8x2-inch baking dish. Cut corned beef in 8 slices; stand slices up in 2 rows in casserole. Top with crumbs. Bake in moderate oven (375°) for 25 minutes or till hot. Serves 8.

MEXI-CHILI CASSEROLE

All the zesty flavors of Mexican enchiladas team up in this speedy casserole—

**1 6-ounce package (about 5 cups) corn
   chips
8 ounces sharp process American
   cheese, shredded (2 cups)
1 15-ounce can (1⅔ cups) chili with
   beans
1 15-ounce can (1⅔ cups) enchilada
   sauce
1 8-ounce can (1 cup) tomato sauce
1 tablespoon instant minced onion
1 cup dairy sour cream**

Reserve 1 cup of the corn chips and ½ cup of the cheese. Combine remaining chips and cheese with the chili, enchilada sauce, tomato sauce, and onion. Pour into 11x7x1½-inch baking dish. Bake uncovered in moderate oven (375°) for 30 minutes or till thoroughly heated. Spread top with sour cream; sprinkle with reserved cheese. Ring remaining corn chips around edge. Bake 5 minutes longer. Makes 6 servings.

SWISS LUNCHEON SPECIAL

**2 cups sliced onion
2 tablespoons butter or margarine
6 hard-cooked eggs, sliced
8 ounces natural Swiss cheese,
   shredded (about 2 cups)
    . . .
1 10½-ounce can condensed cream of
   chicken or cream of celery soup
¾ cup milk
Dash pepper
6 slices French bread, ½ inch thick,
   buttered**

Cook onion in butter till tender but not brown. Spread in bottom of 10x6x1½-inch baking dish. Reserve 6 egg slices for garnish, top onion with remaining eggs, then with cheese. Mix soup, milk, and pepper; heat, stirring, till smooth.

Pour sauce over casserole, being sure some goes to bottom. Place bread slices on top, overlapping them a little. Bake in moderate oven (350°) for 25 to 30 minutes or till heated through. Place in broiler a few minutes, if necessary to toast bread. Makes 6 servings.

BAKED CHEESE FONDUE

Old-time favorite fondue with a new twist—pour it all in one dish and bake to perfection—

> 1 cup milk, scalded
> 1½ cups soft bread crumbs
> 8 ounces sharp process American
>   cheese, shredded (2 cups)
> ½ teaspoon dry mustard
> ¼ teaspoon salt
> Dash pepper
> 3 slightly beaten egg yolks
>   . . .
> 3 stiff-beaten egg whites

Combine milk, crumbs, cheese, mustard, salt, pepper, and egg yolks. Fold in egg whites. Pour into ungreased 10x6x1½-inch baking dish. Bake in slow oven (325°) about 35 to 40 minutes or till firm. Makes 6 servings.

SWISS RICE SOUFFLE

> ¾ cup uncooked rice
> 2 cups milk
>   . . .
> 6 tablespoons butter or margarine
> 3 tablespoons all-purpose flour
> 1½ teaspoons salt
> 2 cups milk
> 8 ounces natural Swiss cheese, shredded
>   (about 2 cups)
>   . . .
> 4 egg yolks
> 4 egg whites

Cook rice uncovered in 2 cups milk over low heat till tender (about 15 minutes), stirring frequently with a fork. When all milk is absorbed, remove from heat.

Melt butter; blend in flour and salt. Add 2 cups milk. Cook, stirring constantly, till smooth and bubbly. Remove from heat. Add cheese. Stir until cheese is melted. Add rice.

Beat egg yolks till thick and lemon-colored. Fold cheese mixture into yolks; cool slightly. Beat egg whites to stiff peaks; fold yolk mixture into whites. Pour into *ungreased* 1½-quart souffle dish or casserole. Bake in moderate oven (350°) for 65 minutes or till knife inserted halfway between center and edge comes out clean. Serve immediately. Makes 6 servings.

SCALLOPED BACON AND EGGS

A luncheon special—bacon and eggs with cheese—

> ¼ cup chopped onion
> 2 tablespoons butter or margarine
> 2 tablespoons all-purpose flour
> 1½ cups milk
> 4 ounces sharp process American
>   cheese, shredded (1 cup)
> 6 hard-cooked eggs, sliced
> 1½ cups crushed potato chips
> 10 to 12 slices bacon, crisp-cooked
>   and crumbled

Cook onion in butter till tender, but not brown; blend in flour. Add milk. Cook, stirring constantly, till mixture thickens and bubbles. Add cheese; stir till melted.

Place a layer of egg slices in 10x6x1½-inch baking dish. Cover with *half* the cheese sauce, *half* the potato chips, and *half* the bacon. Repeat layers. Bake in moderate oven (350°) for 15 to 20 minutes or till hot through. Serves 4.

CLASSIC CHEESE STRATA

> 8 slices day-old bread
> 8 ounces sharp process American
>   cheese, sliced
>   . . .
> 4 eggs
> 2½ cups milk
> ½ teaspoon prepared mustard
> 1 tablespoon chopped onion
> 1½ teaspoons salt
> Dash pepper

Trim crusts from 5 slices of the bread; cut in half diagonally. Use trimmings and remaining 3 slices *untrimmed* bread to cover bottom of 8- or 9-inch square baking dish. Top with cheese.

Arrange the 10 trimmed "triangles" in 2 rows atop the cheese. (Points should overlap bases of preceding "triangles.") Beat eggs; blend in milk, mustard, onion, salt, and pepper; pour over bread and cheese.

Cover with waxed paper; let stand 1 hour at room temperature or several hours in refrigerator. Bake in slow oven (325°) for 1 hour or till knife inserted halfway between center and edge comes out clean. Let stand 5 minutes before serving to firm. Makes 6 servings.

The calm, collected way of entertaining guests for dinner relies on a wonderful make-ahead recipe such as Company Strata. A flavorful combination of cheese, broccoli, and ham is topped with bread "doughnuts and holes" and a mustard sauce. (You'll have nicer edges if you freeze the bread before cutting into "doughnuts.") Store the Strata covered in the refrigerator to blend flavors. You can even make it a day ahead! An hour before company comes, pop it in the oven. For a pretty finish, sprinkle with shredded cheese last 5 minutes of baking.

Company Strata: From 12 slices white bread cut 12 "doughnuts and holes." Fit the scraps of bread (top crusts removed) in bottom of 13x9x2-inch baking dish. Layer 12 ounces sharp process cheese, sliced, one 10-ounce package frozen chopped broccoli, cooked and drained, and 2 cups diced fully cooked ham over bread. Arrange "doughnuts and holes" atop. Combine 6 slightly beaten eggs, 3½ cups milk, 2 tablespoons instant minced onion, ½ teaspoon salt, and ¼ teaspoon dry mustard; pour over bread. Cover; refrigerate 6 hours. Bake uncovered at 325° for 55 minutes. *Let stand 10 minutes before cutting.* Serves 12.

Classic Macaroni And Cheese. Cook 1½ cups elbow macaroni using package directions; drain. Melt 3 tablespoons butter; blend in 3 tablespoons flour. Add 2 cups milk; cook and stir till thick. Add ½ teaspoon salt, dash pepper, ¼ cup minced onion, and 2 cups shredded sharp process cheese; stir till cheese melts. Mix sauce with macaroni. Turn into 1½-quart casserole. Sprinkle tomato slices with salt; arrange on top. Bake at 350° for about 45 minutes. Sprinkle with paprika. Makes 6 to 8 servings.

MACARONI AND SAUSAGE BAKE

1 pound bulk pork sausage
½ cup chopped onion
½ 7-ounce package (1 cup)
  elbow macaroni
1 10½-ounce can condensed cream of
  celery soup
⅔ cup milk
3 slightly beaten eggs
4 ounces sharp process American
  cheese, shredded (1 cup)
¾ cup corn flakes, crushed
1 tablespoon butter or margarine,
  melted

Cook sausage and onion till lightly browned.
Drain off excess fat. Cook macaroni according
to package directions; drain. Combine sausage
mixture, macaroni, soup, milk, eggs, and
cheese. Place in 8x8x2-inch baking dish. Mix
corn flakes and butter; arrange over casserole.
Bake at 350° for 40 minutes. Serves 6.

MEAT 'N MACARONI SUPPER

1 medium onion, chopped (½ cup)
2 tablespoons butter or margarine,
  melted
1 10½-ounce can condensed cream of
  celery soup
1 7½- or 8-ounce can (1 cup) tomatoes,
  cut up
¼ teaspoon thyme
Dash pepper
    . . .
½ 7-ounce package (1 cup) elbow
  macaroni, cooked and drained
1 12-ounce can luncheon meat, cut in
  1x½-inch strips
¼ cup chopped green pepper
    . . .
2 ounces sharp process American
  cheese, shredded (½ cup)

In medium skillet, cook onion in butter or margarine till tender but not brown. Stir in the
soup, tomatoes, thyme, and pepper. Add the
cooked macaroni, luncheon meat, and green
pepper. Spoon into a 1½-quart casserole. Top
with shredded cheese. Bake, uncovered, in
moderate oven (350°) for 35 to 40 minutes or
till heated through. Makes 4 to 6 servings.

SALMON MACARONI

½ 7-ounce package (1 cup) elbow
  macaroni
¼ cup butter or margarine
3 tablespoons all-purpose flour
½ teaspoon salt
Dash pepper
¼ teaspoon garlic salt
1¾ cups milk
1 12-ounce carton (1½ cups) cream-
  style cottage cheese
4 ounces sharp process American
  cheese, shredded (1 cup)
1 1-pound can (2 cups) salmon, drained
  and flaked
2 beaten eggs
1½ cups soft bread crumbs
2 tablespoons butter, melted

Cook macaroni using package directions; drain.
Melt butter; blend in flour and seasonings. Add
milk; cook and stir till thick. Add cheeses, salmon, and macaroni. Stir in eggs. Pour into
greased 11x7x1½-inch baking dish.

Toss crumbs in the melted butter; sprinkle
over casserole. Bake at 350° about 30 minutes
or till set in center. Makes 8 servings.

TUNA-SPAGHETTI BAKE

½ 7-ounce package (1 cup) spaghetti
1 6½- or 7-ounce can (1 cup) tuna,
  flaked
¼ cup chopped canned pimiento
¼ cup slivered almonds (optional)
1 tablespoon butter or margarine
1 10½-ounce can condensed cream of
  mushroom soup
½ cup milk
4 ounces sharp process American
  cheese, shredded (1 cup)
½ cup crushed potato chips

Break spaghetti in 1-inch pieces; cook in boiling salted water until tender; drain. Combine
spaghetti with tuna and pimiento. Brown almonds in butter; stir in soup, milk, and cheese.
Heat and stir till cheese melts. Pour over spaghetti; mix well. Pour into 1½-quart casserole.
Border with crushed potato chips. Bake at
350° for 30 minutes. Garnish with pimiento.
Serves 4 or 5.

CREAMY MACARONI AND CHEESE BAKE

Cook 2 cups elbow macaroni according to package directions; drain. Combine with ⅓ cup mayonnaise or salad dressing, ¼ cup chopped canned pimiento, ¼ cup chopped green pepper, and ¼ cup finely chopped onion.

Blend together one 10½-ounce can condensed cream of mushroom soup, ½ cup milk, and ½ cup shredded sharp process American cheese. Stir into macaroni; place in a 1½-quart casserole. Top with additional ½ cup shredded sharp process American cheese. Bake, uncovered, at 400° for 20 to 25 minutes. Serves 4 to 6.

CHICKEN MACARONI CASSEROLE

Cook 1 cup elbow macaroni according to package directions; drain. Combine macaroni with 2 cups diced cooked chicken, 1 cup shredded process American cheese, one 10½-ounce can condensed cream of chicken soup, 1 cup milk, one 3-ounce can broiled mushroom crowns, drained, and ¼ cup chopped pimiento.

Pour mixture into a greased 2-quart casserole. Bake in a moderate oven (350°) for 50 to 60 minutes. Top with an additional ½ cup shredded process American cheese; return to oven till cheese melts. Makes 6 to 8 servings.

Creamy Macaroni and Cheese Bake—so downright good, and so easy to prepare. No wonder it's become a family favorite. Rich, creamy, golden cheese spiced with onion, green pepper, pimiento, and mushroom flavor, coats each piece of macaroni inside and out. Pop this casserole dish in the oven and it's ready by the time you've set the table and tossed a crisp vegetable salad.

COMPANY TUNA BAKE

4 ounces (1 cup) elbow macaroni
1 3-ounce package cream cheese,
  softened
1 10½-ounce can condensed cream of
  mushroom soup
1 6½- or 7-ounce can tuna, drained
  and flaked
1 tablespoon chopped canned pimiento
1 tablespoon chopped onion
1 teaspoon prepared mustard
⅓ cup milk
½ cup dry bread crumbs
2 tablespoons butter or margarine,
  melted

Cook macaroni using package directions; drain. With electric mixer, blend cheese and soup; stir in next 5 ingredients and macaroni. Turn into a 1½-quart casserole. Mix crumbs and butter or margarine; sprinkle over tuna mixture. Bake at 375° for 20 minutes. Serves 4 or 5.

INSIDE-OUT RAVIOLI

1 pound ground beef
1 medium onion, chopped (½ cup)
1 clove garlic, minced
1 tablespoon salad oil
1 10-ounce package frozen chopped
  spinach
1 1-pound can spaghetti sauce with
  mushrooms
1 8-ounce can (1 cup) tomato sauce
1 6-ounce can (⅔ cup) tomato paste
½ teaspoon salt
1 7-ounce package (2 cups) shell or
  elbow macaroni, cooked
4 ounces sharp process American
  cheese, shredded (1 cup)
½ cup soft bread crumbs
2 well beaten eggs
¼ cup salad oil

Brown first 3 ingredients in the 1 tablespoon salad oil. Cook spinach according to package directions. Drain, reserving liquid; add water to make 1 cup. Stir spinach liquid and next 5 ingredients into meat mixture. Simmer 10 minutes. Combine spinach with remaining ingredients; spread in 13x9x2-inch baking dish. Top with meat sauce. Bake at 350° for 30 minutes. Let stand 10 minutes. Serves 8 to 10.

BAKED LASAGNE

1 pound Italian sausage, bulk pork
  sausage, or ground beef
1 clove garlic, minced
1 tablespoon parsley flakes
1 tablespoon basil
1½ teaspoons salt
1 1-pound can (2 cups) tomatoes
2 6-ounce cans (1⅓ cups) tomato
  paste
10 ounces lasagne or wide noodles
3 cups cream-style cottage cheese
2 beaten eggs
1 teaspoon salt
½ teaspoon pepper
2 tablespoons parsley flakes
½ cup grated Parmesan cheese
1 pound Mozzarella or American
  cheese, sliced *very thin*

Brown meat slowly; spoon off excess fat. Add next 6 ingredients. Simmer uncovered about 30 minutes to blend flavors, stirring occasionally.

Cook noodles in boiling salted water till tender; drain; rinse in cold water. Meanwhile combine cottage cheese with eggs, seasonings, and Parmesan cheese. Place *half* the cooked noodles in a 13x9x2-inch baking dish; spread *half* of the cottage-cheese mixture over; add *half* of the Mozzarella cheese and *half* of the meat sauce. Repeat layers. Bake in moderate oven (375°) for 30 minutes. If desired, garnish with triangles of Mozzarella cheese. Let stand 10 to 15 minutes before cutting in squares— filling will set slightly. Serves 8 to 10.

LAZY-DAY LASAGNE

6 ounces lasagne or wide noodles
¼ teaspoon oregano
1 15½-ounce can spaghetti sauce with
  meat
1 cup cream-style cottage cheese
1 6-ounce package sliced Mozzarella
  cheese

Cook noodles using package directions. Drain. Combine oregano with spaghetti sauce.

In a greased 10x6x1½-inch baking dish, alternate layers of noodles, cottage cheese, Mozzarella cheese slices, and spaghetti sauce. Bake at 375° about 30 minutes. Serves 4.

Cheese and eggs: royal fare

SWISS PIE

1 cup (26 crackers) fine cracker crumbs
1/4 cup butter or margarine, melted
6 slices bacon
1 cup chopped onion
2 slightly beaten eggs
3/4 cup dairy sour cream
1/2 teaspoon salt
Dash pepper
8 ounces natural Swiss cheese,
    shredded (2 cups)
1/2 cup shredded sharp process cheese

Combine cracker crumbs and butter; press onto bottom and sides of 8-inch pie plate. Cook bacon till crisp; drain on paper towels; crumble. Pour off all but 2 tablespoons bacon fat; add onion and cook till tender but not brown.

Combine crumbled bacon, onions, eggs, sour cream, salt, pepper, and Swiss cheese. Pour into pie shell. Sprinkle process cheese atop.

Bake in moderate oven (375°) for 25 to 30 minutes, or till knife inserted halfway between the center and edge of filling comes out clean. Garnish with parsley and onion rings. Let stand 5 to 10 minutes before cutting. Serves 4 to 6.

Swiss Pie exemplifies an epicurean masterpiece. Elegant Swiss cheese, enriched by sour cream and subtly flavored with onion, bakes to golden perfection in a crisp crust. Leisurely dining will enable your guests to savor every delicate forkful of this superb specialty.

QUICHE LORRAINE

1 9-inch unbaked pastry shell
8 slices bacon, diced
8 ounces natural Swiss cheese,
  shredded (2 cups)
1 tablespoon all-purpose flour
½ teaspoon salt
Dash nutmeg
3 beaten eggs
1½ cups milk

Bake unpricked pastry shell in very hot oven (450°) *only 5 minutes*, or till lightly browned. Remove from oven; reduce temperature to 325°.

Cook bacon till crisp; drain and crumble; reserve 2 tablespoons. Place remaining bacon in pie shell; add cheese. Combine remaining ingredients; pour over. Trim with reserved bacon.

Bake at 325° for 35 to 40 minutes or till knife inserted just off-center comes out clean. *Let cool 10 minutes before serving.* Serves 6.

CHEESED SCRAMBLED EGGS

Mix 6 beaten eggs with ⅓ cup light cream, ¾ teaspoon salt, and dash pepper. Melt 2 tablespoons fat in skillet; add eggs. Cook, stirring frequently, till eggs begin to set; sprinkle with ¼ cup shredded sharp process American cheese. Continue cooking just till eggs firm and cheese melts. Trim with 2 tablespoons chopped green onion tops. Makes 6 servings.

CHEESE FRENCH OMELET

4 well beaten eggs
3 tablespoons milk
¼ teaspoon salt
Dash *each* pepper and garlic salt
Dash curry powder
2 tablespoons butter or margarine
½ cup diced sharp process cheese

Combine eggs, milk, salt, pepper, garlic salt, and curry powder. Melt butter in 8-inch skillet; when hot, add egg mixture. Cook over medium heat, running spatula around edge and lifting to allow uncooked eggs to flow underneath. When bottom is set and golden, top with cheese. Remove from heat; cover pan 3 minutes. Fold in half; slip onto warm plate. Serves 2 or 3.

PARMESAN OMELET

4 egg yolks
4 egg whites
¼ cup water
¼ cup grated Parmesan cheese

. . .

1 tablespoon butter or margarine
1 recipe Cheddar Cheese Sauce

Beat yolks till very thick. Wash beater. Beat egg whites till frothy; add water. Beat till stiff but not dry. Fold yolk mixture into whites. Fold in Parmesan cheese.

Melt butter in 10-inch oven-going skillet; heat till sizzling hot. Pour in omelet mixture. Reduce heat; cook slowly for about 5 minutes till puffed and golden on bottom. Then bake in slow oven (325°) for 6 to 8 minutes or till knife inserted in center comes out clean.

Loosen sides of omelet with spatula. Make shallow crease across omelet at right angles to skillet handle, just above center. Slip spatula under large half nearer handle. Tilt pan. Fold upper (large) half over lower half. Tip omelet onto heated platter. Serves 2 or 3.

Cheddar Cheese Sauce: Melt 4 teaspoons butter. Blend in 4 teaspoons flour and dash salt. Add ¾ cup milk. Cook, stirring constantly, till thick. Remove from heat; add ¾ cup shredded sharp natural Cheddar cheese; stir to melt. Spoon over omelet.

COUNTRY BLINTZE

6 eggs
⅓ cup milk
½ teaspoon salt
Dash pepper
2 tablespoons butter or margarine
1 8-ounce carton (1 cup) large-curd,
  cream-style cottage cheese
1 to 2 tablespoons chopped green
  onions

Beat eggs slightly; beat in milk and seasonings. Heat butter in 10-inch skillet; pour in omelet mixture and cook slowly. Run spatula around edge, lifting to allow uncooked portion to flow underneath. When egg is just cooked but still shiny on top, loosen edge. Place cheese in center of omelet; top with onion; roll edges over.

Slip onto a warm platter. Serves 3 or 4.

Bring on golden Cheese Souffle, puffed to perfection, and as a cook, you're immediately in the gourmet circle! A souffle rich with cheese, yet cloud-light—tastes as marvelous as it looks.

For top hat: trace circle with teaspoon 1 inch from edge and 1 inch deep.

For high souffle collar: Measure waxed paper with 1 inch overlap around dish; fold in thirds lengthwise; butter one side. Fasten collar with tape or pins around dish with buttered side in and extending 2 inches above top of dish. After baking, remove collar.

CHEESE SOUFFLE

¼ cup butter or margarine
¼ cup all-purpose flour
1 cup milk
½ teaspoon salt
Dash cayenne
8 ounces sharp process American
    cheese, thinly sliced

. . .

4 egg yolks
4 stiff-beaten egg whites

Melt butter; blend in flour and seasonings. Add milk, all at once; cook over medium heat, stirring, till mixture thickens and bubbles. Remove from heat. Add cheese; stir till cheese melts.

Beat egg yolks till very thick and lemon-colored. Slowly add cheese mixture, stirring constantly; cool slightly. Gradually pour over beaten egg whites, folding together thoroughly. Pour into *ungreased* 1½-quart souffle dish or casserole. For a top hat (it puffs in the oven), trace a circle through mixture 1 inch from edge and 1 inch deep. Bake in slow oven (300°) for 1 hour and 15 minutes, or till knife comes out clean. Immediately break apart into servings with 2 forks. Makes 4 servings.

If desired, serve with Shrimp Sauce. Follow directions for Shrimp Sauce given in the recipe Shrimp-curried Eggs on this page.

EASY CHEESE SOUFFLE

Double cheese flavor and double quick, too—

1 11-ounce can condensed Cheddar
    cheese soup
4 ounces sharp process American
    cheese, shredded (1 cup)
4 egg yolks
4 stiff-beaten egg whites

In saucepan, combine soup and cheese. Cook and stir over low heat till cheese melts. Remove from heat. Beat egg yolks till thick and lemon-colored. Slowly add cheese mixture to beaten egg yolks, stirring constantly. Fold cheese mixture into egg whites. Pour into *ungreased* 2-quart souffle dish or casserole.

Bake in slow oven (300°) for 1 hour or till knife inserted comes out clean. Serve immediately. Makes 4 to 6 servings.

TAPIOCA CHEESE SOUFFLE

3 tablespoons quick-cooking tapioca
1 teaspoon salt
1 cup milk
3 egg yolks, slightly beaten
4 ounces sharp process American
    cheese, shredded (1 cup)
¼ teaspoon Worcestershire sauce
3 stiff-beaten egg whites

Combine tapioca, salt, and milk; bring to boil, stirring constantly. Add small amount hot mixture to egg yolks; return to hot mixture and cook till thickened (about 1 minute). Add cheese and Worcestershire; stir till cheese is melted. Fold into egg whites. Pour into *ungreased* 1½-quart casserole or souffle dish.

Bake in slow oven (325°) for 35 to 40 minutes or till knife inserted comes out clean. Serve immediately. Makes 6 servings.

SHRIMP-CURRIED EGGS

8 hard-cooked eggs
⅓ cup mayonnaise or salad dressing
½ teaspoon salt
¼ to ½ teaspoon curry powder
½ teaspoon paprika
¼ teaspoon dry mustard

Shrimp Sauce:
2 tablespoons butter or margarine
2 tablespoons all-purpose flour
1 10-ounce can frozen condensed cream
    of shrimp soup
1 soup can milk
2 ounces sharp process American
    cheese, shredded (½ cup)

. . .

1 cup soft bread crumbs
2 tablespoons butter or margarine,
    melted

Cut eggs in half lengthwise; remove yolks and mash; mix with next 5 ingredients. Refill egg whites; arrange in 10x6x1½-inch baking dish.

Make **Shrimp Sauce:** Melt 2 tablespoons butter; blend in flour. Stir in soup and milk; cook and stir till thick. Add cheese; stir to melt.

Cover eggs with sauce. Mix crumbs and melted butter; sprinkle around edge. Bake in moderate oven (350°) for 15 to 20 minutes or till heated through. Serves 6 to 8.

South of the border specialties

Mexican cuisine offers an array of specialties grand for entertaining. Guests enjoy cheese-topped Enchiladas and puffy omelet-like Chilies Rellenos con Queso surrounding Mexican steaks and fried rice at the center of the platter.

CHILES RELLENOS CON QUESO

**3 fresh long green hot peppers or
   canned green peeled chiles
4 to 6 ounces sharp natural Cheddar
   cheese, shredded (1 to 1½ cups)
All-purpose flour
6 egg whites
3 tablespoons all-purpose flour
Dash salt
6 egg yolks**

Cut peppers or canned chiles in half crosswise. (To prepare *fresh* peppers, place on broiler pan; broil 4 inches from heat just till skins blister. Cool slightly. Peel and carefully remove the stems and seeds.) Stuff each pepper or chile half with cheese; roll in flour. Beat egg whites till stiff, but not dry. Add 3 tablespoons flour and the salt to yolks; beat till thick and lemon-colored; fold into whites.

For each Chile Relleno, spoon a mound (about ½ cup) of egg batter into shallow hot fat (375°); spread batter into a circle. As batter begins to set, gently top each mound with a cheese-stuffed pepper. Cover with more batter. Continue cooking till underside is browned. Turn carefully and brown second side; drain on absorbent paper. Serve at once. Serves 6.

CHEESE ENCHILADAS

Wash 1 pound dried whole red chiles or 6 ounces (about 3⅓ cups) dried seeded red chiles thoroughly. If not already seeded, stem chiles, slit and remove seed veins and seeds. Wash again. Cover with cold water; bring to vigorous boil. Drain and wash again. Put chiles through food chopper, then through a sieve. Stir in 1 clove garlic, crushed, ¼ teaspoon crushed oregano, pinch comino (cumin seed), and ¼ cup salad oil. To one 10½-ounce can condensed beef broth or 1¼ cups bouillon, add water to make 2¾ cups; add to chile mixture and simmer for 20 minutes. Salt the chile mixture to taste.

Heat ½ cup salad oil in a skillet, and when hot, fry 8 tortillas*, one at a time, on both sides. (Fry only till they puff a bit, but don't crisp or brown.) After each tortilla is fried, dip it in the chile mixture (have it in another skillet), then place on a platter.

Have at hand 3 cups shredded sharp natural Cheddar cheese, 1 medium onion, chopped fine, and ½ cup chopped ripe olives. *Reserve 1 cup* of the cheese. Place a handful (about ¼ cup) of cheese on each tortilla and sprinkle with onion and olives. Roll up each tortilla and place in greased shallow baking pan. (Now the tortillas have become enchiladas, and may be kept in readiness for baking at this stage.)

Half an hour before serving time, pour rest of the chile mixture over enchiladas; sprinkle with reserved 1 cup cheese. Bake in moderate oven (350°) for 25 minutes. Makes 8 servings. *Note:* You can buy tortillas frozen or canned.

Chiles Rellenos con Queso are airy fried omelets with a cheese-stuffed pepper tucked inside. A mound of egg batter cooks in shallow hot fat. When set, a cheese-filled pepper is placed atop, then another mound of batter is spooned over. After turning, tongs are handy for removal from pan.

Prize pizza

HOMEMADE PIZZA CRUST

Soften 1 package active dry yeast in 1 cup warm water. Beat in 1½ cups all-purpose flour; mix in 1 tablespoon olive oil and 1 teaspoon salt. Stir in 2 cups additional all-purpose flour. Knead till smooth and elastic, about 12 minutes (will be firm). Place in lightly oiled mixing bowl; turn oiled side up. Cover. Let rise in warm place till more than double, 1½ to 2 hours. Punch down, cover and chill till cold.

Cut dough in 2 parts. On lightly floured surface, roll each in 12-inch circle, about ⅛ inch thick. Place on greased baking sheets or two 12-inch pizza pans, turning edges of dough up slightly. With knuckles, dent dough here and there to prevent bubbles from forming.

Brush each circle with 1 tablespoon olive oil. Fill with desired filling. Bake in hot oven (425°) for 20 to 25 minutes, or till crust is done. Makes two 12-inch pizzas.

JIFFY PIZZA CRUST

Prepare 1 package hot roll mix according to package directions, but using *1 cup* warm water and *no egg. Do not let rise.* Cut in 2 parts.

With oiled hands, pat each part into a 12-inch circle on oiled baking sheets or into two 12-inch pizza pans. Clip edge at 1-inch intervals; press so it stands up. Brush circles with olive oil. Fill with desired filling. Bake in very hot oven (450°) for 15 to 20 minutes, or till crust is done. Makes two 12-inch pizzas.

Crispy crusts and imaginative fillings make up these tantalizing pizzas. For pizza-in-a-hurry, start with jiffy crust or packaged pizza, spread with canned pizza sauce, then add your own fix-ups! For salami pizza, sprinkle bits of salami atop, shake Parmesan cheese over all. Trim with salami cornucopias. Anchovy pizza sports triangles of Mozzarella cheese and a spiral of anchovies. Using these ideas as starters, dream up your own special toppers! Classic pizza lovers can make Pepperoni, Sausage, or Mushroom Pizza from scratch.

MUSHROOM PIZZA

Using one 6-ounce package sliced Mozzarella cheese, cut each slice in 4 triangles. Reserve 8 triangles; layer remainder over two 12-inch pizza-dough circles. Top with ½ cup chopped onion, ¼ cup chopped green pepper, and one 3-ounce can broiled sliced mushrooms, drained.

Season; drizzle with one 10-ounce can pizza sauce; dash with crushed oregano. Top each with 4 cheese triangles and pickled banana peppers. Bake as directed for crust. Makes 2 pizzas.

SAUSAGE PIZZA

In skillet, break 1 pound Italian sausage in bits. Cook slowly until lightly browned, 10 minutes, stirring occasionally; drain off fat.

Drain one 1-pound can tomatoes, reserving ½ cup juice. Cut tomatoes in small pieces and layer on two 12-inch pizza-dough circles. Sprinkle with salt and pepper; then cover with one 6-ounce package Mozzarella cheese, *thinly sliced* and torn in pieces. Drizzle with olive oil (1 tablespoon per pizza). Sprinkle with sausage.

Combine one 6-ounce can tomato paste, reserved tomato juice, 2 cloves garlic, minced, 1 tablespoon crushed oregano, and 1 tablespoon whole basil. Mix well; spread over sausage. Dash generously with salt and pepper. Scatter ¼ cup grated Parmesan or Romano cheese atop. Drizzle with olive oil (1 tablespoon per pizza). Bake as for crust. Makes two pizzas.

PEPPERONI PIZZA

Slice ¾ pound small pepperoni, *thinly;* reserve 20 slices. Scatter remainder over two 12-inch pizza-dough circles. Sprinkle with ¼ cup grated Parmesan or Romano cheese. Combine two 8-ounce cans tomato sauce, 1 tablespoon crushed oregano, 1 teaspoon anise seed, and 4 cloves garlic, crushed; mix; spread over pizzas. Top with one 6-ounce package Mozzarella cheese, *thinly* sliced and torn in pieces. Sprinkle with ¼ cup grated Parmesan or Romano cheese. Trim with reserved pepperoni. Bake as for crust. Makes two pizzas.

Saucy specials

FONDUE LORE

Swiss Cheese Fondue holds the mystique of complicated cookery. Yet this subtle-flavored delicacy is created from simple ingredients in minutes. Anyone can master the easy techniques of careful simmering and constant stirring. Gear includes only a chafing dish or casserole on a heating unit, a wooden fork for silent stirring, and long-handled forks for dipping.

In this friendly ritual, folks all dip from the same fondue pot and help with the cooking to boot. Each guest dunks a piece of crusty French bread, speared on a long-handled fork, in the melted cheese, gives it a swirl and withdraws a morsel of cheese-coated bread. Through the joint effort of guests, this chain dipping keeps the fondue continuously in motion. (The Swiss stir with big swoops all in one direction.)

Oops! The first one to drop his bread in the pot gives a kiss to the friend of his choice. And don't forget the crusty cheese in the bottom of the pot—it's a gourmet's special treat.

CLASSIC CHEESE FONDUE

    12 ounces natural Swiss cheese, cut in
        thin julienne strips (3 cups)
    1 tablespoon all-purpose flour
    1 clove garlic, halved
    1¼ cups sauterne
    Dash freshly ground pepper
    Dash nutmeg
    3 tablespoons dry sherry
    French bread or hard rolls, torn in
        bite-size pieces, each with one crust

Toss cheese with flour to coat. Rub inside of fondue cooker vigorously with cut surface of garlic. Pour in sauterne and warm just till air bubbles start to rise. (Don't cover or boil.)

Remember *to stir all the time from now on*: add a handful of cheese; when melted, toss in another handful. After all cheese is blended in and is bubbling *gently*, stir in seasonings and sherry. Spear bread cube on long-handled fork and dip into cheese. (If fondue becomes thick, add a little *warmed* sauterne.) Serves 5 or 6.

BLENDER CHEESE FONDUE

    8 ounces Gruyere cheese, diced (2 cups)
    2 cups dry white wine
    1 pound natural Swiss cheese, diced
        (4 cups)
    1½ tablespoons all-purpose flour
    ¼ teaspoon nutmeg
    ¼ teaspoon freshly ground pepper
    1 clove garlic
    French bread or hard rolls, torn in bite-
        size pieces, each with one crust

Place Gruyere cheese in blender container; cover and blend at high speed 20 seconds. Scrape down sides. Blend 10 seconds more or till cheese is in tiny bits; remove from blender.

Warm the wine without covering or boiling. Put *2 cups* of the Swiss cheese in blender along with flour, nutmeg, pepper, and garlic. Cover; blend at high speed 20 seconds. Scrape down sides; blend 10 seconds more or till cheese is in tiny pieces. Keeping blender at low speed, pour in warm wine and gradually add remaining 2 cups of Swiss cheese. Blend smooth.

Pour wine-Swiss cheese mixture into saucepan. Add the blended Gruyere cheese. Cook and stir over low heat till smooth and thick, about 15 minutes. Pour into chafing dish; keep warm. Spear French bread cubes on forks and dip into the melted cheese. Makes 10 servings.

ROSY CHEESE FONDUE

    8 ounces sharp process American
        cheese, diced (1½ cups)
    2 ounces blue cheese (½ cup)
    1 teaspoon Worcestershire sauce
    ½ cup condensed cream of tomato
        soup
    2 tablespoons sherry
    Toasted French bread cubes

In heavy saucepan, combine cheeses, Worcestershire, and soup. Cook over low heat, stirring constantly, till smooth. Stir in wine. Keep hot over warm water in chafing dish. Spear bread on forks; dip in cheese. Makes 1 cup.

Cheese Fondue features nutty-flavored Swiss cheese and wine generously coating crunchy bites of French bread. Our Swiss friends say to skip the salad, and no cold drink, please. Offer steaming mugs of fragrant apple juice or freshly brewed coffee. Dessert? Make it fruit.

CLASSIC CHEESE RABBIT

8 ounces sharp process American
   cheese, shredded (2 cups)
¾ cup milk
1 teaspoon dry mustard
1 teaspoon Worcestershire sauce
Dash cayenne
1 well beaten egg

Heat cheese and milk over *very low heat*, stirring
constantly till cheese melts and sauce is smooth.
Add seasonings. Add small amount hot mixture
to egg; return to hot mixture. Stir over *very low
heat* till mixture thickens and is creamy. Serve
over toast. Makes 4 servings.

CHEESE RABBIT

2 11-ounce cans condensed Cheddar
   cheese soup
½ cup beer
¼ teaspoon Worcestershire sauce
Dash dry mustard
5 or 6 slices French bread, about ¾-
   inch thick, toasted
5 or 6 slices bacon, halved and crisp-
   cooked
5 or 6 thick tomato slices
1 3-ounce can broiled mushroom
   crowns, drained (½ cup)

In a saucepan, combine soup, beer, Worcestershire sauce, and mustard. Stir to blend. Simmer
over low heat 10 minutes, stirring frequently.

Place toasted bread slices in shallow 13x9x2-
inch baking dish. Top *each* with 2 pieces bacon,
a tomato slice, and 2 or 3 mushroom crowns.
Pour cheese sauce over all. Broil 3 to 4 inches
from heat till cheese bubbles (about 3 minutes).
Makes 5 or 6 servings.

QUICK CHEESE RABBIT

Combine one 10½-ounce can condensed
cream of mushroom soup and 8 ounces sharp
process American cheese, shredded (2 cups), in
top of double boiler. Heat over simmering water till cheese melts, stirring occasionally. Add
¼ cup sliced ripe olives and ¼ cup chopped
green pepper. Serve over hot chowmein noodles,
toast, or rye bread. Serves 4 or 5.

GOLDEN VELVET RABBIT

In a saucepan, melt ¼ cup butter or margarine; blend in ¼ cup all-purpose flour, ½ teaspoon salt, and dash pepper. Add 1¾ cup milk
all at once; cook stirring constantly till mixture
thickens and bubbles. Remove from heat; add
¾ cup shredded process American cheese
spread, and ¾ cup shredded Muenster cheese;
stir to melt cheeses. Stir in 2 tablespoons
chopped canned pimiento, and ¼ teaspoon
Worcestershire sauce. Makes 2⅓ cups sauce.

Serve over **Bacon Waffles:** Use bacon drippings as shortening in your favorite waffle recipe. Sprinkle cooked bacon bits over batter just
before closing lid of waffle baker.

DOUBLE CHEESE RABBIT

Melt 3 tablespoons butter; blend in 3 tablespoons all-purpose flour. Add 1¾ cups milk;
cook, stirring constantly till mixture thickens
and bubbles. Remove from heat; add ½ cup
shredded sharp process cheese and ½ cup
shredded process Swiss cheese. Stir to melt.

Add ½ teaspoon Worcestershire sauce, 2
cups diced fully cooked ham, one 3-ounce can
broiled sliced mushrooms, drained (½ cup),
and 2 tablespoons chopped canned pimiento.
Heat through. Serve over hot toast points or
freshly baked cornbread. Makes 4 to 6 servings.

MEXICAN RABBIT

2 tablespoons chopped green pepper
2 tablespoons butter or margarine
1 8-ounce can (1 cup) tomatoes
8 ounces sharp process American
   cheese, shredded (2 cups)
1 1-pound 4-ounce can (2½ cups)
   whole kernel corn, drained
1 well beaten egg
½ cup soft bread crumbs
Dash salt
¼ teaspoon chili powder

Cook green pepper in butter till tender. Add
tomatoes and cheese; stir till cheese melts.
Combine corn and egg; add to tomato mixture.
Add bread crumbs, salt, and chili powder. Heat
through, stirring constantly. Serve piping hot
on toast points. Makes 6 servings.

Main dishes starring meat and cheese

VEAL PARMIGIANO

3 tablespoons butter or margarine
½ cup corn flake crumbs
¼ cup grated Parmesan cheese
½ teaspoon salt
Dash pepper

. . .

1 pound veal cutlets or veal steak,
   about ¼ inch thick*
1 slightly beaten egg

. . .

1 8-ounce can (1 cup) tomato sauce
½ teaspoon crushed oregano
½ teaspoon sugar
Dash onion salt
2 thin slices Mozzarella cheese,
   halved (about 4 ounces)

Melt butter in 10x6x1½-inch baking dish. Combine corn flake crumbs, Parmesan cheese, salt, and pepper. Cut veal in serving pieces; dip in egg, then in crumb mixture. Place in baking dish. Bake in hot oven (400°) for 20 minutes. Turn meat; continue baking 15 to 20 minutes or till tender.

Meanwhile, combine tomato sauce, oregano, sugar, and onion salt; heat just to boiling, stirring frequently. Pour sauce over meat. Top with cheese. Return to oven to melt cheese, about 3 minutes. Makes 4 servings.

*If meat is thicker than ¼ inch, pound thin.

CHEESE ROUND STEAK

Coat one 2-pound beef round steak, ½ inch thick, with a mixture of ¼ cup flour, ½ teaspoon salt, and ¼ teaspoon garlic salt. Pound meat ¼ inch thick; cut in 6 to 8 pieces.

In skillet, brown meat slowly in 3 tablespoons hot shortening. Add 1 cup hot water and ¼ cup chopped onion. Cover; simmer 1 hour or till meat is tender. Sprinkle with ½ cup shredded sharp process American cheese and 2 tablespoons snipped parsley. Cover and heat to melt cheese. Makes 6 to 8 servings.

CHEESE-STUFFED PORK CHOPS

4 1-inch pork chops
1 3-ounce can chopped mushrooms
4 ounces process Swiss cheese, diced
   (¾ cup)
¼ cup snipped parsley
½ cup fine dry bread crumbs
¼ teaspoon salt
Dash pepper
1 beaten egg

Trim excess fat from chops. Cut a pocket in fat side of each chop. Drain mushrooms, reserving liquid. Combine mushrooms, cheese, parsley, and ½ teaspoon salt; stuff into pockets; toothpick and lace shut. Mix crumbs, salt, and pepper. Dip chops in egg, then crumbs. Slowly brown chops in hot fat. Add reserved mushroom liquid; cover and simmer 1 hour or till chops are done. Remove chops. *Gravy:* Blend 2 tablespoons flour and ¼ cup cold water to a smooth paste; gradually stir into liquid in skillet. Cook and stir till thick. Serves 4.

SWISS VEAL FOLDOVERS

6 veal cutlets
6 square slices process Swiss cheese
6 square slices boiled ham
2 tablespoons all-purpose flour
¼ teaspoon paprika
2 tablespoons fat
1 10½-ounce can condensed cream of
   mushroom soup
1 cup light cream
¼ cup cooking sauterne

Pound each veal slice to a very thin rectangle (about 8x4 inches). Cut cheese and ham slices in half; stack alternately in center of each veal cutlet. Fold veal over to cover cheese and ham; roll carefully in mixture of flour and paprika. Brown in hot fat. Mix remaining ingredients; add to skillet. Cover; simmer, stirring occasionally, 30 minutes or till tender. Serves 6.

FAMILY SKILLET SUPPER

¼ cup butter or margarine
3 cups loose-pack frozen hash-brown
   potatoes
¼ cup chopped onion
¼ cup chopped green pepper
4 slightly beaten eggs
1 12-ounce can luncheon meat
½ cup shredded sharp process cheese

In 10-inch skillet, melt butter. Add potatoes, onion, and green pepper; season. Stir to combine. Cover; cook over low heat 15 minutes, stirring occasionally. Pour eggs evenly over top. Cut meat in ¾x3½-inch sticks; arrange in spokes atop. Cover; cook over low heat 10 minutes till eggs set. Top with cheese; cover till melted. Cut in wedges. Makes 5 or 6 servings.

SAUCY MEATBALL SUPPER

1½ pounds ground beef
½ cup chopped onion
2 eggs
¼ cup milk
1 cup (2 slices) soft bread crumbs
2 tablespoons snipped parsley
½ teaspoon dried oregano, crushed
1 11-ounce can condensed Cheddar
   cheese soup
¼ cup dry white wine

Mix first 7 ingredients, 1 teaspoon salt, and dash pepper; mix well. Shape in 1-inch balls. In large skillet, brown meatballs in shortening. Drain excess fat. Combine soup, ½ cup water, and wine. Add to meat. Simmer, covered, 15 to 20 minutes. Serve over hot spaghetti. Serves 6.

Family Skillet Supper takes 30 minutes—that's total preparation time, and it's all in one skillet! Frozen hash-brown potatoes spiked with onion form the crispy base. Eggs poured on top lend an omelet effect, while spokes of meat and melted cheese add the tasty finishing touch.

MEAT LOAF—ITALIAN STYLE

1 cup medium saltine cracker crumbs
  (20 crackers)
1½ pounds ground beef
1 6-ounce can (⅔ cup) tomato paste
2 eggs
1 medium onion, finely chopped
¼ cup finely chopped green pepper
¾ teaspoon salt
Dash pepper
1 12-ounce carton (1½ cups) small-curd
  cream-style cottage cheese
1 3-ounce can broiled chopped mushrooms, drained (½ cup)
1 tablespoon snipped parsley
¼ teaspoon oregano

Set aside ½ cup of the cracker crumbs. Combine remaining crumbs with next 7 ingredients; mix well. Pat half the mixture in bottom of 8x8x2-inch baking pan. Combine reserved crumbs with remaining ingredients; spread evenly over meat in pan. Top with remaining meat mixture. Bake at 350° for 1 hour. Let stand 10 minutes before serving. Serves 8.

STUFFED ROLLED RIB ROAST

¼ cup chopped onion
1 clove garlic, minced
1 tablespoon brown sugar
1 teaspoon salt
Dash pepper
1 teaspoon prepared mustard
1 teaspoon Worcestershire sauce
1 cup soft bread crumbs (1½ slices)
1 3- to 4-pound rolled beef rib roast
1 3-ounce can broiled sliced mushrooms, drained (½ cup)
2 tablespoons chopped stuffed green
  olives
2 ounces sharp process American
  cheese, shredded (½ cup)

Combine first 8 ingredients with ¼ cup water. Unroll roast and spread with bread mixture; sprinkle with remaining ingredients. Reroll roast and tie securely; fasten ends with skewers. Place on rack in shallow baking pan. Roast at 325° to desired doneness, allowing 1½ to 2 hours for rare, 1¾ to 2¼ hours for medium, or 2 to 2½ hours for well-done. Serves 9 to 12.

MINUTE STEAK ROLLS

Pound 6 minute steaks if thick; season lightly. Drain one 3-ounce can broiled chopped mushrooms, reserving liquid. Sprinkle mushrooms, ½ cup snipped parsley, ½ cup chopped onion, and ½ cup grated Parmesan cheese over the minute steaks.

Starting at narrow end, tightly roll up each steak; fasten with toothpicks. In skillet, brown rolls *slowly* in 2 tablespoons hot fat. Add *half* of a 10½-ounce can condensed beef broth. Cover; simmer 30 to 45 minutes or till tender.

Remove steaks to hot platter. Combine 2 tablespoons cornstarch, reserved mushroom liquid, and remaining broth; stir into skillet. Cook, stirring till thick. Spoon over meat; sprinkle with grated Parmesan cheese. Serves 6.

CHEESE-FILLED MEAT LOAF

1½ pounds ground beef
1 8-ounce can (1 cup) tomato sauce
¾ cup quick-cooking rolled oats
¼ cup chopped onion
1 egg
1 tablespoon Worcestershire sauce
1½ teaspoons salt
1½ teaspoons monosodium glutamate
¾ to 1 teaspoon oregano
¼ teaspoon pepper
1 6-ounce package sliced Mozzarella
  cheese

Combine all ingredients except cheese; mix well. Divide meat mixture in thirds. Pat ⅓ in bottom of 9½x5x3-inch loaf pan; cover with *half* the cheese. Repeat layers, ending with meat. Bake at 350° for 1 hour. Serves 5 or 6.

PINWHEEL BURGERS

Combine 1½ pounds ground beef, ⅓ cup milk, 1 egg, ½ cup fine saltine cracker crumbs (10 crackers), ¼ cup minced green pepper, ¼ cup minced onion, 1 tablespoon prepared mustard, ½ teaspoon salt, and dash pepper.

On waxed paper, pat to a 12-inch square shape. Spread with one 5-ounce jar process blue-cheese spread *or* pimiento-cheese spread. Roll meat as for jellyroll; seal edge. Cut in twelve 1-inch slices. Broil 12 to 14 minutes, turning once, or till done. Makes 6 servings.

Chicken and turkey with cheese

Serve Rolled Chicken Washington for a truly elegant meal. It started as a specialty of one of the country's major air lines. Whole chicken breasts are boned and flattened, then wrapped around a cheese and mushroom mixture to make neat little packages. When served, these crispy golden brown rolls are fork tender. One bite reveals the steamy cheese surprise inside.

ROLLED CHICKEN WASHINGTON

½ cup finely chopped fresh mushrooms
2 tablespoons butter or margarine
2 tablespoons all-purpose flour
½ cup light cream
¼ teaspoon salt
Dash cayenne pepper
5 ounces sharp natural Cheddar cheese, shredded (1¼ cups)
6 or 7 boned whole chicken breasts
All-purpose flour
2 slightly beaten eggs
¾ cup fine dry bread crumbs

Cook mushrooms in butter, about 5 minutes. Blend in flour; stir in cream. Add seasonings; cook and stir till mixture is very thick. Stir in cheese; cook over very low heat, stirring, till cheese melts. Turn into pie plate. Cover; chill 1 hour. Cut firm cheese mixture into 6 or 7 pieces; shape into short sticks.

Remove skin from chicken breasts. Place each piece, boned side up, between clear plastic wrap. (Overlap meat where split.) Pound out from the center with wood mallet to form cutlets not quite ¼ inch thick. Peel off wrap. Sprinkle meat with salt. Place a cheese stick on each piece. Tucking in the sides, roll as for jellyroll. Press to seal well. Dust rolls with flour; dip in egg, then in crumbs. Cover and chill thoroughly—at least 1 hour.

An hour before serving, fry rolls in deep, hot fat (375°) for 5 minutes or till golden brown; drain on paper towels. Bake in shallow baking dish at 325° for 30 to 45 minutes. Serves 6 or 7.

CHEDDAR TURKEY CASSEROLE

Prepare 1 cup packaged precooked rice using package directions, adding 2 tablespoons instant minced onion to the boiling water. Fluff cooked rice with fork and spread in greased 10x6x1½-inch baking dish. Sprinkle with one cup frozen green peas, thawed, then cover with 4 to 6 slices (or 2 cups diced) cooked turkey.

Blend together one 11-ounce can condensed Cheddar cheese soup and 1 cup milk; pour evenly over turkey. Combine 1 cup finely crushed rich round cheese crackers and 3 tablespoons butter, melted; sprinkle atop. Bake at 350° for 35 minutes. Makes 4 to 6 servings.

THREE CHEESE CHICKEN BAKE

8 ounces lasagne noodles
1 recipe Mushroom Sauce
1½ cups cream-style cottage cheese
3 cups diced cooked chicken
8 ounces process American cheese, shredded (2 cups)
½ cup grated Parmesan cheese

Cook noodles till tender in large amount boiling salted water. Drain; rinse in cold water. *Mushroom sauce:* Cook ½ cup *each* chopped onion and green pepper in 3 tablespoons butter; stir in one 10½-ounce can condensed cream of chicken soup, ⅓ cup milk, one 6-ounce can broiled sliced mushrooms, drained, ¼ cup chopped pimiento, and ½ teaspoon basil.

Place *half* the noodles in a 13x9x2-inch baking dish; cover with *half each* of the mushroom sauce, cottage cheese, chicken, process cheese, and Parmesan cheese. Repeat layers. Bake at 350° for 45 minutes. Serves 8 to 10.

CHICKEN-RICE DIVAN

2 10-ounce packages frozen broccoli spears
½ cup shredded Parmesan cheese
6 large slices cooked chicken *or* 2 cups cubed chicken
Salt and pepper
1 cup cooked rice
2 tablespoons butter or margarine
2 tablespoons all-purpose flour
1 cup milk
1 tablespoon lemon juice
1 cup dairy sour cream

Cook broccoli according to package directions; drain. Arrange in 11x7x1½-inch baking dish. Sprinkle with half the shredded Parmesan cheese; top with chicken. Season with salt and pepper; spoon on cooked rice. Prepare a medium white sauce: Melt butter or margarine in saucepan over low heat. Blend in flour; add milk all at once. Cook over medium heat, stirring constantly, till mixture thickens and bubbles; remove from heat. Stir in lemon juice; gently fold in sour cream and pour over chicken in casserole. Sprinkle with remaining Parmesan cheese. Bake in hot oven (400°) for 15 to 20 minutes or till lightly browned. Makes 6 servings.

Sea food favorites

SEA-FOOD CASSEROLE

2 tablespoons butter or margarine
2 tablespoons all-purpose flour
1/4 teaspoon salt
1 cup milk
1/2 cup shredded sharp process cheese
12 medium shrimp, cooked and split
   or 1 4½-ounce can shrimp
1½ cups fresh lump crab meat or 1
   7½-ounce can crab meat
1 cup steamed lobster or 1 5½-ounce
   can lobster
1 3-ounce can broiled sliced mushrooms, drained (½ cup)
2 tablespoons sherry
1 tablespoon lemon juice
Dash bottled hot pepper sauce
1/4 teaspoon Worcestershire sauce
1/2 cup shredded sharp process cheese
1 cup soft bread crumbs
2 tablespoons butter or margarine,
   melted

Melt butter over low heat. Blend in flour and salt. Add milk all at once. Cook quickly, stirring constantly, till sauce thickens and bubbles; remove from heat. Add ½ cup cheese and stir till melted. Add next 8 ingredients; mix well. Place mixture in a 1-quart casserole. Sprinkle cheese over. Combine crumbs and melted butter; sprinkle over cheese. Bake in a 375° oven for 40 minutes. Serves 4 to 6.

GOLDEN SHRIMP BAKE

Trim, butter, and cube 8 slices slightly dry bread (5 cups cubed). Shred 8 ounces sharp process cheese (2 cups shredded). Place *half* the bread cubes in greased 11x7x1½-inch baking dish. Add 2 cups cleaned cooked or canned shrimp, one 3-ounce can broiled sliced mushrooms, drained (½ cup), and *half* the cheese. Top with remaining bread cubes and cheese. Beat together 3 eggs, ½ teaspoon *each* salt and dry mustard, dash pepper, and dash paprika; add 2 cups milk; pour over casserole. (May be refrigerated.) Bake at 350° for 45 to 50 minutes till just set. Serves 5 or 6.

CRAB 'N MUSHROOMS MORNAY

2 6-ounce cans broiled mushroom
   crowns, drained (2 cups)*
1 6½- to 7¾-ounce can (about 1 cup)
   crab meat, flaked
2 teaspoons lemon juice
3 tablespoons butter or margarine
3 tablespoons all-purpose flour
1½ cups milk
2 slightly beaten egg yolks
6 ounces sharp process American
   cheese, shredded (1½ cups)
2 tablespoons sherry

Arrange mushrooms, hollow side up, in 8-inch round baking dish. Cover with crab meat; sprinkle with lemon juice. Melt butter in saucepan; blend in flour. Add milk all at once; cook and stir till mixture thickens and bubbles. Add small amount of hot mixture to egg yolks; return to sauce and cook 1 minute. Remove from heat; stir in 1¼ *cups of the cheese* and the sherry. Pour sauce over crab; sprinkle with 1/4 cup cheese. Bake at 350° for 20 minutes or till very hot. Serve over toast points. Serves 6.

*Or use 2 pints fresh mushrooms. Wash. Remove stems; arrange in baking dish.

OYSTER PUDDING

6 slices white bread
3 tablespoons butter or margarine,
   softened
1/2 8-ounce package (4 slices) sliced
   sharp process American cheese
1 pint oysters with liquid
2 slightly beaten eggs
3 cups milk
1 teaspoon salt
1/4 teaspoon pepper

Spread bread with butter, cut in cubes. Place *half* the cubes in bottom of 11x7x1½-inch baking dish. Arrange cheese over. Add oysters and liquid; top with remaining bread cubes. Combine eggs, milk, salt, and pepper; pour over all. Bake at 325° for 1¼ hours or till knife inserted off center comes out clean. Serves 4 to 6.

Toasted Cheese Bowl. Cut crust from top and sides of 1 unsliced loaf of bread. Make long horizontal slit 1 inch from bottom of loaf, extending to within 1 inch of other end.

Leaving 1 inch around all sides, cut a rectangle straight down from top to slit. Lift out. Place loaf on greased baking sheet.

Blend 4 tablespoons soft butter or margarine with one 5-ounce jar sharp cheese spread. Spread over top, sides, and inside of loaf. Bake at 400° for 10 to 12 minutes. Fill with your favorite shrimp or tuna salad. To serve, spoon salad onto plates, then slice loaf. Makes 5 or 6 servings.

DIPS, SPREADS, AND TIDBITS

Dips and spreads provide popular fare for every occasion. Smooth cottage and cream cheese, sharp Cheddar, nutty-flavored Swiss, nippy blue, and mild Edam or Gouda spike the many scrumptious recipes. Some are plain, others fancy, but all are delicious! Suggested dippers offer more variety—crusty bread, crisp crackers, potato or corn chips, and assorted fresh fruits.

Tempting tidbits hit the spot anytime. You'll find jiffy snacks for quick fix-ups as well as dressy ones for more elaborate entertaining. Try miniature pizzas for the kids and serve your bridge club shrimp and pimiento cheese tucked inside a flaky turnover.

Dream of dunking a crispy shredded wheat wafer into piping-hot Cheese 'n Crab Dip—tastes like whipped fondue with tender morsels of crab! You'd never guess it was made in minutes. Sound tempting? Serve this elegant dip at your next party and you'll have compliments galore! Garnish with parsley and crab.

Dips and spreads superb

HOT CHEESE 'N CRAB DIP

1 6½- or 7½-ounce can crab meat
1 10-ounce stick sharp natural Cheddar cheese
1 8-ounce package sliced sharp process American cheese
¼ cup butter or margarine
½ cup sauterne

Reserving a few pieces for garnish, shred crab meat. Cut cheese in small pieces; combine in a saucepan with the butter and sauterne. Stir over low heat till cheeses melt. Stir in the shredded crab meat and continue cooking to heat through. Pour into chafing dish; garnish with reserved crab meat pieces. Serve with shredded-wheat wafers, or chunks of crusty bread and use fondue forks. Makes 3 cups.

CHEDDAR DIP

Great appetizer, snack, or non-sweet dessert—

8 ounces sharp natural Cheddar cheese
⅓ cup light cream
1 teaspoon prepared mustard

Let cheese come to room temperature; cut in cubes. Add cream and mustard. Beat with electric mixer or blender until almost smooth. Cut unpared apples in slices; arrange around bowl of cheese dip. Makes about 1¼ cups dip.

BLUE-CHEESE DIP

4 ounces blue cheese, crumbled (1 cup)
1 3-ounce package cream cheese, softened
2 tablespoons milk
2 tablespoons mayonnaise

Combine all ingredients and beat with electric mixer until mixture is light and fluffy, or use electric blender. Serve with cherry-tomatoes as dippers—spear the tiny tomatoes on toothpicks and anchor in cucumber as base.

LOW-CALORIE DIP

1 12-ounce carton (1½ cups) cream-style cottage cheese
1 tablespoon mayonnaise
1 teaspoon salad-spice-and-herb mix

In electric blender or mixer, blend all ingredients until almost smooth. Chill. Garnish with snippets of parsley. Pass celery and carrot sticks. Makes about 1½ cups dip.

DIP AWAY DIET DIP

Beat one 12-ounce carton (1½ cups) small-curd cream-style cottage cheese, 1½ teaspoons instant minced onion, and ½ teaspoon seasoned salt with electric mixer. Chill. Stir in 1 tablespoon finely chopped canned pimiento or snipped parsley. Serve with relish sticks.

CREAMY BLUE CHEESE DIP

1 8-ounce carton (1 cup) cream-style cottage cheese
2 3-ounce packages cream cheese, softened
2 tablespoons crumbled blue cheese
1 small clove garlic
Few drops bottled hot pepper sauce

Pour ¼ cup water into blender. Add cottage cheese; cover and blend at high speed about 20 seconds. Add remaining ingredients. Cover; blend 30 seconds or till smooth. Makes 2 cups.

DRIED BEEF LOG

Blend together one 8-ounce package cream cheese, softened, ¼ cup grated Parmesan cheese, and 1 tablespoon prepared horseradish; stir in ⅓ cup chopped stuffed green olives.

On waxed paper, shape in two 6-inch rolls, 1½ inches in diameter. Chill several hours or overnight. Roll "logs" in 1 cup snipped dried beef. Slice and serve with crisp crackers.

CHUTNEY CHEESE SPREAD

2 3-ounce packages cream cheese,
  softened
4 ounces sharp natural Cheddar cheese,
  shredded (1 cup)
4 teaspoons dry sherry
½ teaspoon curry powder
¼ teaspoon salt
½ cup finely chopped chutney
1 tablespoon finely snipped chives or
  green onion tops

Blend thoroughly cheeses, sherry, and seasonings. Spread on flat serving platter, shaping a layer ½-inch thick. Chill till firm. To serve; spread chutney over top; sprinkle with chives; surround with wheat crackers.

THREE CHEESE SPREAD

Combine 2 cups shredded sharp natural Cheddar cheese, 4 ounces blue cheese, crumbled, and one 3-ounce package cream cheese, softened. Serve with crackers. Makes 2 cups.

ANCHOVY-CHEESE DIP

1 8-ounce package cream cheese,
  softened
2 tablespoons chopped green olives
1 tablespoon anchovy paste
1 tablespoon snipped green onion tops
  or chives
1 tablespoon milk
1 teaspoon lemon juice
¼ teaspoon Worcestershire sauce

Combine all ingredients in small mixer bowl. Beat at medium speed till light and fluffy. Chill till ready to serve. Makes 2 cups.

FESTIVE EDAM

Have 1 round Edam or Gouda cheese at room temperature. Cut slice off top of cheese. Scoop out center leaving ¼-inch wall. Scallop edge of cheese shell, using a biscuit cutter as guide. Whip the cheese with electric mixer or mash with fork. Beat in enough light cream to make of spreading consistency. Mound cheese in shell. Serve at room temperature.

These "dipper dandies" star as tempting snacks for TV-munchers or when friends drop in for a visit. Spur-of-the-moment dunkers could include fresh fruits, in season, crisp relishes, chips, or crackers. For **Cheese Fluff:** blend some whipped cream cheese with tangy fruit juice. **Jiffy Dip** is a blend of one 8-ounce roll braunschweiger, 1 cup dairy sour cream, and ½ package blue cheese salad-dressing mix; chill.

Appetizer Cheese Mousse: Soften *2 teaspoons* unflavored gelatin in ¼ cup cold water. Place over boiling water and stir till gelatin dissolves. Stir gelatin into 2 cups dairy sour cream. Add 2 teaspoons Italian salad-dressing mix, ¼ cup crumbled blue cheese, and one 8-ounce carton (1 cup) small-curd cream-style cottage cheese. Beat with electric or rotary beater till well blended. Pour into 3½-cup ring mold or small loaf pan. Chill till firm; unmold and garnish.

BEAN-CHEESE DIP

Beans and chili powder lend a Mexican touch—

In saucepan or chafing dish, combine one 11½-ounce can condensed bean with bacon soup and one 6-ounce roll garlic-flavored cheese food, diced. Heat, stirring constantly, till cheese melts. Stir in 1 cup dairy sour cream, ¼ cup minced onion, and ¼ teaspoon bottled hot pepper sauce. Heat through (do not boil).

Dash with chili powder. Pass with assorted chips and crackers. Makes 2⅔ cups dip.

CLAM-CHEESE DIP

Combine one 8-ounce package cream cheese, softened, ½ cup crumbled blue cheese, 1 tablespoon snipped chives or green onion tops, ¼ teaspoon salt, and bottled hot pepper sauce to taste. Beat mixture until smooth.

Drain one 7½-ounce can minced clams, reserving liquor. Stir clams into cheese mixture. Add enough reserved clam liquor (or milk) to make of spreading consistency. Keep chilled; remove from refrigerator 15 minutes before serving. Pass crackers or chips. Makes 1⅔ cups.

LOBSTER DIP ELEGANTE

1 8-ounce package cream cheese
¼ cup mayonnaise or salad dressing
1 clove garlic, crushed
1 teaspoon grated onion
1 teaspoon prepared mustard
1 teaspoon sugar
Dash seasoned salt
1 5-ounce can (about 1 cup) lobster,
    flaked
3 tablespoons cooking sauterne

Melt cream cheese over low heat, stirring constantly. Blend in mayonnaise, garlic, onion, mustard, sugar, and salt. Stir in lobster and sauterne; heat through. Serve hot with melba toast and assorted crackers. Makes 1¾ cups.

HOT CHEESE DIP WITH FRUIT

In a small saucepan or chafing dish, place one 6-ounce can (⅔ cup) evaporated milk, 1 cup shredded sharp process American cheese, 1 cup shredded process Swiss cheese, 1 tablespoon prepared mustard, 1 teaspoon Worcestershire sauce, and dash bottled hot pepper sauce.

Cook over low heat, stirring until cheeses melt and mixture is smooth. Remove from heat; stir in ¼ cup finely chopped canned pimiento. Serve hot as dip for apple or pear wedges.

CHILI CHEESE LOG

1 3-ounce package cream cheese
8 ounces sharp process American
    cheese, shredded (2 cups)
1 tablespoon lemon juice
¼ teaspoon garlic powder
Dash red pepper
¼ cup finely chopped pecans
1 teaspoon chili powder
1 teaspoon paprika

Let cheeses stand at room temperature to soften; combine cheeses, lemon juice, garlic powder, and red pepper; beat with electric or rotary beater till light and fluffy. Stir in nuts. Shape in a roll about 1½ inches across. Sprinkle roll with mixture of chili powder and paprika. Chill. Before serving, let stand at room temperature 10 minutes. Slice and serve with crackers.

OLIVE-CHEESE BALL

1 8-ounce package cream cheese,
    softened
8 ounces blue cheese, crumbled (2 cups)
¼ cup butter or margarine, softened
1 4½-ounce can chopped ripe olives,
    well drained (⅔ cup)
1 tablespoon snipped chives
⅓ cup chopped California walnuts or
    toasted diced almonds

Blend cheeses and butter. Stir in olives and chives. Chill slightly for easier shaping. Form in ball on serving dish. Chill thoroughly. Just before serving, sprinkle chopped nuts over ball. Serve with assorted crackers. Makes 3 cups.

SHRIMP-CHEESE FONDUE

1 10-ounce can frozen condensed cream
    of shrimp soup
½ cup milk
8 ounces natural Swiss cheese, shredded
    (2 cups)
1 tablespoon sherry
2 teaspoons instant minced onion
¼ teaspoon dry mustard

Heat soup and milk till blended. Stir in cheese, sherry, onion, and mustard. Cook and stir over low heat till cheese melts. Serve immediately in chafing dish with relishes and toasted bread triangles for dunking. Makes 2 cups.

TUNA PATE

1 8-ounce package cream cheese,
    softened
2 tablespoons chili sauce
2 tablespoons snipped parsley
1 teaspoon instant minced onion
¼ teaspoon bottled hot pepper sauce
Few drops Worcestershire sauce
2 7-ounce cans tuna

Blend cream cheese, chili sauce, parsley, onion, hot pepper sauce, and Worcestershire sauce; gradually add tuna. Beat until thoroughly blended. Pack into small (1-quart) bowl. Chill thoroughly. Unmold; top with capers and serve with assorted crackers. Makes 3 cups.

Tidbits to tempt you

PICCOLO PIZZAS

½ pound Italian sausage
1 teaspoon crushed oregano
1 clove garlic, minced
1 package refrigerated biscuits
½ to 1 6-ounce can (⅓ to ⅔ cup)
  tomato paste
4 ounces sharp process American
  cheese, shredded (1 cup)
¼ cup grated Parmesan cheese

Brown sausage slowly, stirring to crumble; spoon off excess fat, then stir in oregano and garlic. Place biscuits on a greased baking sheet. With bottom of floured custard cup, make a hollow in each, 4 inches in diameter (leave rim). Fill with tomato paste and sausage. Sprinkle with American cheese, then with Parmesan. Bake in 425° oven 10 minutes. Makes 10.

CHEESE-STUFFED MUSHROOMS

2 6-ounce cans broiled mushroom
  crowns*, drained (2 cups)
1 tablespoon finely chopped onion
1 teaspoon salad oil
¼ cup finely chopped salami
¼ cup smoke-flavored cheese spread
1 tablespoon catsup
Fine soft bread crumbs

Hollow out mushroom crowns and chop enough pieces to make 3 tablespoons; cook pieces with onion in oil. Stir in next 3 ingredients. Stuff into mushroom crowns; sprinkle with crumbs. Bake on baking sheet in hot oven (425°) for 6 to 8 minutes or till hot.

*Or use 2 pints fresh mushrooms. Wash; trim off tips of stems. Remove stems and chop enough to make ¼ cup. Continue as above.

PARMESAN SHOESTRINGS

Empty 1 can shoestring potatoes into a shallow baking dish. Sprinkle with ½ cup grated Parmesan cheese. Heat at 350° till toasty.

CHEESE STICKS

2 sticks pie crust mix
4 ounces sharp natural Cheddar cheese,
  shredded (1 cup)
¼ teaspoon dry mustard
2 teaspoons paprika

Prepare pie crust mix according to package directions. Stir in remaining ingredients till mixture forms a ball. Roll out on floured surface to 16x12x¼-inch rectangle. Cut into sticks ½ inch wide and 4 inches long. Place on ungreased baking sheet. Bake in hot oven (425°) for 10 to 12 minutes or till golden brown. Remove from baking sheet; cool. Makes 96 sticks.

HIBACHI CHEESE BISCUITS

Cut refrigerated biscuits (from a tube) in thirds, and roll each piece into a ball. Dip in melted butter or margarine, then in grated Parmesan cheese. String on skewers, leaving about ½ inch between balls. "Bake" over *hot* coals, *turning constantly*, until browned and completely done, about 7 minutes. Eat right now! One tube of biscuits makes 30.

SAUSAGE BITES

4 ounces sharp process American
  cheese, shredded (1 cup)
¼ cup butter or margarine, softened
¾ cup all-purpose flour
½ teaspoon paprika
¼ teaspoon salt
5 links brown-and-serve sausage

Blend cheese with butter. Stir in flour, paprika and salt. Mix well. Brown sausage in skillet and cut each link into 4 pieces. Wrap just enough dough around each piece of sausage to cover completely. Bake on ungreased baking sheet in hot oven (400°) for 10 to 15 minutes or until golden brown. Serve hot. Makes 20.

Olive Bites: Substitute 36 stuffed green olives for sausage. Proceed as above. Makes 36.

SHRIMP CHEESE TURNOVERS

½ cup butter or margarine
1 3-ounce package cream cheese,
  softened
1 cup sifted all-purpose flour
1 5-ounce jar pimiento-cheese spread
1 4½-ounce can shrimp, drained

Cut butter and cream cheese into flour till mixture resembles coarse crumbs. Gather dough
into ball; chill 1 hour. Roll ⅛-inch thick on
floured cloth; cut with 2-inch round cutter.
Dot rounds with cheese spread and cut-up
shrimp pieces. Fold over into half circle; seal
edges. Bake on ungreased baking sheet at 375°
for 15 minutes or till golden. Makes 3 dozen.

SWISS-FRANK ROLL-UPS

2 17-ounce packages cocktail
  frankfurters
8 ounces natural Swiss cheese, cut in
  2x¼x¼-inch strips
1 8-ounce tube refrigerated biscuits,
  quartered
2 tablespoons butter or margarine,
  melted
2 tablespoons sesame seeds

Cut lengthwise slit in frankfurters, not quite
through; fill with strips of cheese. Shape biscuit
quarters into 4x¾-inch rectangles. Wind dough
around frankfurters. Place on foil-covered baking sheet. Brush tops of biscuit with melted
butter; sprinkle with sesame seeds. Bake at
400° for 10 minutes or till browned. Makes 40.

SWISS SANDWICH PUFFS

16 slices tiny "icebox" rye bread
½ cup mayonnaise or salad dressing
¼ cup finely chopped onion
2 tablespoons snipped parsley
8 slices process Swiss cheese

Toast bread on both sides. Combine mayonnaise, onion, and parsley; spread on toast. Cut
out rounds of cheese to fit toast; place a cheese
round atop each slice, covering mayonnaise
mixture. Broil 3 to 4 inches from heat till cheese
is puffy and golden, 2 to 3 minutes. Makes 16.

BROILED OLIVE CANAPES

10 slices white bread
2 tablespoons butter or margarine,
  softened
4 ounces sharp process American
  cheese, shredded (1 cup)
½ cup chopped stuffed green olives
2 stiff-beaten egg whites
3 slices bacon, finely diced

With 2-inch round cutter, cut 20 bread rounds.
Place on broiler rack and toast on both sides.
Butter one side. Fold cheese and olives into
egg whites; spoon on buttered rounds; sprinkle
with bacon. Top each with an olive slice. Broil
4 to 5 inches from heat for 5 to 8 minutes or till
cheese melts. Makes 20.

FRENCH-FRIED CAMEMBERT

Cut six 1⅓-ounce triangles of Camembert*
in half lengthwise, then crosswise (24 pieces).
Shape cheese crust around soft center so it
covers as much of center as possible. Dip in
beaten egg, then in fine dry bread crumbs, then
again in egg and crumbs. (Crumbs prevent the
cheese from leaking through.)

Fry in deep hot fat (375°) till crumbs are
crisp and golden brown. Drain and serve hot on
small plates. Offer picks or forks.

*Or use Port du Salut. Cut in bite-size pieces
or cut with melon-ball cutter; mold into small
balls. Coat and fry.

TOASTY CHEESE PINWHEELS

Unsliced sandwich loaf
8 ounces sharp process American
  cheese, shredded (2 cups)
½ cup mayonnaise or salad dressing
2 teaspoons lemon juice
2 teaspoons prepared mustard
1 teaspoon salt

Cut bread in lengthwise slices ¼ inch thick.
Trim crusts from bread. Combine cheese with
remaining ingredients. Spread each long slice
with the cheese mixture. Roll as for jelly roll,
beginning at narrow end. Wrap in foil and chill.
For pinwheels, cut in ¼- to ½-inch slices.
Broil 2 minutes or till golden. Makes 56.

BREADS AND SANDWICHES

Bake a batch of cheese bread and the heavenly aroma will bring your family on the run.

Greats from the griddle include grilled cheese favorites such as ham 'n cheese and Reubens plus many new adventures!

Broil or bake a sandwich so cheese melts to perfection.

Stack a hearty sandwich with your favorite cheeses, meats, relishes—whatever is on hand.

Party-going sandwich fancies are served as decorative dainties on occasions when you want something special.

Cheddar Bran Muffins and Cheese Crescents are served warm from the oven with butter curls. They're natural go-withs for cups of steaming coffee.

Bake a batch of cheese bread

CHEDDAR BRAN MUFFINS

1¼ cups buttermilk or sour milk
1 cup whole bran
¼ cup shortening
⅓ cup sugar
1 egg
1½ cups sifted all-purpose flour
1½ teaspoons baking powder
½ teaspoon salt
¼ teaspoon soda
4 ounces sharp natural Cheddar
    cheese, shredded (1 cup)

Pour buttermilk or sour milk over bran in small bowl; let stand till softened. Meanwhile, cream shortening and sugar till light and fluffy. Beat in egg. Sift together flour, baking powder, salt, and soda. Add to creamed mixture alternately with milk-bran mixture. Stir in shredded cheese. Fill greased muffin pans ⅔ full. Bake at 400° for 30 minutes. Serve warm. Makes 12.

AIRY CHEESE ROLLS

1 package active dry yeast
¼ cup *warm* water
1¾ cups milk, scalded
4 ounces sharp process American
    cheese, shredded (1 cup)
¼ cup sugar
2 tablespoons shortening
1 teaspoon salt
4 cups sifted all-purpose flour
1 beaten egg
½ cup corn meal

Soften yeast in warm water. In large bowl of electric mixer, combine milk, cheese, sugar, shortening, and salt. Stir till cheese melts; cool to lukewarm. Add *2 cups* of the flour; beat 2 minutes at medium speed. Add egg, yeast, corn meal, and remaining flour. Beat 2 minutes.

Cover; let rise in warm place till double, about 1¼ hours; stir down. Fill greased 2½-inch muffin pans ½ full. Cover and let rise till double, about 45 minutes. Bake in moderate oven (375°) for 15 to 20 minutes. Makes 2 dozen.

CHEESE CRESCENTS

Serve warm to fully enjoy the melted Cheddar—

2 cups packaged biscuit mix
4 ounces sharp natural Cheddar
    cheese, shredded (1 cup)
2 tablespoons butter or margarine,
    melted

Prepare biscuit mix according to package directions; knead 8 to 10 times. Roll out on floured surface to a 14-inch circle. Brush with melted butter or margarine; sprinkle with cheese; cut in 10 pie-shaped wedges. Starting at wide end, roll up each wedge to form a crescent.

Put crescents, point down, on lightly greased baking sheet. Bake in a very hot oven (450°) about 10 minutes or till golden brown. Remove from baking sheet immediately. Makes 10.

CHEESE LOAF

1 package active dry yeast
¼ cup warm water
½ cup packaged (shaker top) grated
    American cheese
2 tablespoons sugar
1 teaspoon salt
2 tablespoons shortening
¾ cup hot water
3 to 3½ cups sifted all-purpose flour
1 egg

Soften yeast in ¼ cup warm water. Combine next 5 ingredients, stirring to dissolve. Cool to lukewarm. Stir in *2 cups* flour, mixing well. Add yeast and egg; mix well. Add remaining flour or enough to make soft dough. Turn out on lightly floured surface; knead till smooth. Place in lightly greased bowl, turning once. Cover; let rise till double, 1¼ hours.

Punch down; divide in 2 parts. Cover; let rest 10 minutes. Shape each part in roll 12 inches long. Twist together in rope fashion, pinching ends together. Place in greased 9½x 5x3-inch loaf pan. Cover; let rise till double, 1½ hours. Bake at 375° for 35 minutes.

CHEESE BREAD STICKS

1 package hot-roll mix
4 ounces sharp process American
    cheese, shredded (1 cup)
1 tablespoon poppy seed
1/4 cup butter or margarine, melted

Prepare hot-roll dough using package directions; add cheese and poppy seed. After dough rises, divide in half. On lightly floured surface, roll each half to 10x6-inch rectangle, 1/2 inch thick. Cut each in twenty 6-inch-long sticks. (For smooth shape, roll sticks under hand.) Place on greased baking sheet; brush with butter. Let rise till double, 30 to 45 minutes. Bake at 400° for 10 minutes. Makes 40.

PURIS

Cut 2 tablespoons shortening into 2 cups sifted all-purpose flour and 1/2 teaspoon salt. Add 1/2 cup shredded sharp process American cheese. Stir in 1/2 to 2/3 cup water to make soft dough. Knead and pound dough for about 10 to 15 minutes.

Cover; let stand 1/2 hour. Roll *very thin* on lightly floured surface. Cut in 4-inch circles. Fry in deep hot fat (400°) till golden brown, turning once. Drain on paper towels. Keep warm in very slow oven. Makes 12.

OLIVE PIZZA BREAD

1 slightly beaten egg
1 cup pitted ripe olives, cut in pieces
1/3 cup butter or margarine, melted
1 tablespoon instant minced onion
1 teaspoon Worcestershire sauce
Dash bottled hot pepper sauce
8 ounces process American cheese,
    shredded (2 cups)
3 cups packaged biscuit mix
1 cup milk
1 teaspoon caraway seed

Mix egg, olives, butter, onion, Worcestershire, pepper sauce, and cheese. Combine biscuit mix and milk; stir to make soft dough. Spread dough in greased 14-inch pizza pan. Spoon olive topping over dough; sprinkle with caraway. Bake in hot oven (425°) for 20 to 25 minutes.

CHEESE-SOUP BREAD

2 packages active dry yeast
1/2 cup warm water
1 11-ounce can condensed Cheddar
    cheese soup
1/4 cup shortening
2 tablespoons sugar
1 teaspoon salt
2 eggs*
5 1/4 to 5 1/2 cups all-purpose flour

Soften yeast in water. Heat soup to lukewarm; add shortening, sugar, salt, eggs, and yeast mixture. Stir in 2 cups flour; beat well. Add enough of remaining flour to make a moderately stiff dough. Turn out on lightly floured surface and knead in remaining flour till smooth. Shape in a ball; place in lightly greased bowl, turning once. Cover; let rise 1 hour or till double.

Punch down; divide dough in half and let rest 10 minutes covered. Shape in loaves; place in 2 well greased 8 1/2x4 1/2x2 1/2-inch loaf pans. Let rise again 1 hour or till double. Bake in moderate oven (375°) for 30 to 35 minutes.

*For glossy crust, reserve part of one egg white. After shaping loaves, brush tops with egg white; dash with onion or garlic salt.

BACON SPOON BREAD

3/4 cup corn meal
1 1/2 cups cold water
8 ounces sharp natural Cheddar
    cheese, shredded (2 cups)
1/4 cup butter or margarine, softened
2 cloves garlic, crushed
1/2 teaspoon salt
1 cup milk
4 well beaten egg yolks
1/2 pound sliced bacon, crisp-cooked
    and drained
4 stiff-beaten egg whites

Combine corn meal and water; cook, stirring constantly, till consistency of mush. Remove from heat; add next 4 ingredients; stir to melt cheese. Gradually add milk. Stir in egg yolks.

Crumble bacon, reserving some for garnish; add to corn-meal mixture. Fold in egg whites. Pour into greased 2-quart souffle dish. Bake at 325° for 65 minutes or till done. Spoon into warm dishes; top with butter. Serves 6.

ISRAELI CHEESE BLINTZES

Mix ¾ cup sifted all-purpose flour *or* ½ cup matzo meal (cake meal) and ½ teaspoon salt. Combine 1 cup milk and 2 slightly beaten eggs; gradually add to flour, beating till smooth. Pour about 2 tablespoons batter into hot, lightly greased 6-inch skillet; quickly swirl pan to spread batter evenly.

Cook over medium heat till golden on bottom and edges begin to pull away from side, about 2 minutes. Loosen; turn out of skillet; repeat.

For filling: Blend together one 12-ounce carton (1½ cups) well-drained cottage cheese, 1 slightly beaten egg, 2 tablespoons sugar, ½ teaspoon vanilla, and dash cinnamon. Have pancakes cooked-side up; spoon filling in center of each. Overlap sides atop filling; overlap ends.

Brown on both sides in small amount hot fat. Serve hot, topped with sour cream and cherry preserves. Makes 6 or 7 servings (2 each).

Toasted Cheese Loaf: Cut crusts from top and sides of unsliced sandwich loaf. Make 8 slices crosswise *almost* to bottom crust; make one cut lengthwise down center. Place on baking sheet. Blend ¼ cup butter and one 5-ounce jar sharp cheese spread; spread between slices, over top and sides. Tie string around loaf. Bake at 400° for 10 to 12 minutes. Makes 16.

EASY CHEESE BREAD

2½ cups packaged biscuit mix
½ cup *shredded* sharp process
   American cheese
½ cup finely *diced* sharp process
   American cheese
2 teaspoons poppy seed
1 beaten egg
1 cup milk

Combine biscuit mix, cheese, and poppy seed. Add egg and milk; mix just to blend. Beat vigorously 1 minute. Turn into well-greased 8½x4½x2½-inch loaf pan. Sprinkle with additional poppy seed. Bake in moderate oven (350°) about 50 minutes or till done; remove from pan; cool on rack. Serve warm.

BRUNCH BITES

Beat together two 3-ounce packages softened cream cheese, ¼ cup sugar, 1 egg, and ½ teaspoon vanilla; stir in one 8¾-ounce can crushed pineapple, well drained. Flatten rolls from one package of 12 refrigerated butter-flake rolls on ungreased baking sheet to a 3½-inch circle, building up rim on sides. Place 1 tablespoon filling in center of each. Bake at 375° for 12 to 14 minutes; serve warm. Makes 12.

CHEESE-TOPPED BISCUITS

2 packages refrigerated biscuits
4 ounces sharp natural Cheddar
   cheese, shredded (1 cup)
2 tablespoons light cream
½ teaspoon poppy seeds
Dash dry mustard

Arrange 15 biscuits, overlapping, around edge of well greased 9x1½-inch round pan. Overlap remaining biscuits in center. Combine remaining ingredients; crumble atop biscuits. Bake at 425° for 15 minutes. Remove from pan immediately. Serve hot. Makes 8 to 10 servings.
Parmesan Biscuits: Mix ¼ cup melted butter, 2 tablespoons snipped parsley, and 1 clove garlic, minced. Dip 2 packages refrigerated biscuits in butter mixture; arrange in pan as above. Top with remaining butter and ¼ cup grated Parmesan cheese. Bake as above.

Greats from the griddle

HAM 'N CHEESE FRENCH TOAST

Make 6 sandwiches with slices of boiled ham and sharp process American cheese between 2 bread slices. For batter, mix 3 slightly beaten eggs, $\frac{1}{4}$ cup milk, and dash salt. Dip sandwiches in batter. Grill on lightly buttered griddle at high heat till toasty and cheese starts to melt—turn once. Makes 6 sandwiches.

TOASTED SWISS

Fill two slices of white bread with slice of Swiss cheese sprinkled with $\frac{1}{2}$ teaspoon poppy seed. For 4 sandwiches, mix 1 teaspoon minced onion with $\frac{1}{4}$ cup butter; spread on top and bottom of sandwiches. Grill both sides.

BOSTON BEANWICH

For each sandwich, spread a slice of whole-wheat bread with $\frac{1}{4}$ cup drained, canned baked beans in molasses sauce. Crumble 2 slices of crisp-cooked bacon over beans. Top with a slice of sharp process American cheese.

Spread second slice of bread with prepared mustard and add atop, mustard side down. Liberally butter the top and bottom of sandwich. Grill both sides till baked beans are hot through and cheese melts slightly.

GRILLED CHEESE ITALIANO

Top a slice of Italian bread with slice *each* of Mozzarella cheese and salami. Dash on crushed oregano. Top with second slice of bread. Butter top and bottom of sandwich. Grill both sides.

INSIDE-OUT PIZZA

Spread inner surfaces of sandwich with pizza sauce; sprinkle one side with basil and grated Parmesan cheese. Add several slices of Provolone cheese to make generous filling. Brush outer surfaces with soft butter. Grill slowly.

GRILLED REUBEN SANDWICH

12 slices pumpernickel
$\frac{1}{2}$ cup Thousand Island dressing
6 slices Swiss cheese
6 tablespoons drained sauerkraut
$\frac{1}{4}$ to $\frac{1}{2}$ pound cooked or canned corned beef, sliced very thin
Butter or margarine, softened

Spread 6 slices of bread with Thousand Island dressing. Top each with cheese, 1 tablespoon sauerkraut, sliced corned beef, and bread. Butter top and bottom of sandwiches. Grill on both sides till cheese is melted. Makes 6.

TOASTED CRAB SANDWICHES

1 $6\frac{1}{2}$- or $7\frac{1}{2}$-ounce can (about 1 cup) crab meat, drained and flaked
2 ounces sharp process American cheese, shredded ($\frac{1}{2}$ cup)
$\frac{1}{4}$ cup chopped celery
2 tablespoons drained sweet-pickle relish
2 tablespoons chopped green onions
1 hard-cooked egg, chopped
3 tablespoons mayonnaise
$\frac{1}{2}$ teaspoon lemon juice
$\frac{1}{2}$ teaspoon prepared horseradish
10 slices bread, buttered generously
5 tomato slices

Combine crab, cheese, celery, relish, onions, egg, mayonnaise, lemon juice, and horseradish. Spread on *unbuttered* side of 5 bread slices. Add tomato slices; season with salt and pepper. Top with bread slices, buttered side up. Grill on griddle or sandwich grill till sandwiches are golden brown. Makes 5 sandwiches.

JIFFY HAM AND CHEESE

Spread slice of rye bread with sharp cheese spread and another slice with deviled ham from a can. Put sandwich together; butter top and bottom. Grill both sides till toasted.

Broil or bake a sandwich

PIZZA PRONTO

For a pair of pizzas: With palms of hands, flatten two 8-ounce packages refrigerated biscuits to 4½x2-inch ovals. On greased baking sheet, arrange 10 biscuits at slight angles to each other, in two adjoining rows. Press adjoining ends together securely. On another baking sheet, repeat with remaining 10 biscuits.

Combine one 8-ounce can tomato sauce, 1 teaspoon instant minced onion, ¼ teaspoon oregano, and ¼ teaspoon garlic salt; spread over pizzas to within ½ inch of edges. Sprinkle with 1 cup shredded sharp natural Cheddar cheese; top with 2 slices (3 ounces) Mozzarella cheese, torn in pieces.

Arrange one 6-ounce can broiled mushroom crowns, drained, over pizzas. Bake at 450° for 8 to 10 minutes, or till edges of crusts are golden brown. Garnish with ½ cup pitted ripe olives and red and yellow pickled peppers. Makes 2 pizzas, 4 or 5 servings each.

DAD'S DENVERS

Cut one loaf of French bread in half lengthwise; wrap top half and store for later use. Toast bottom half; spread with one 4½-ounce can (⅔ cup) deviled ham.

Combine 4 eggs, ¼ cup milk, ¼ teaspoon salt, and dash pepper; beat thoroughly. Add ¼ cup chopped green onions. Heat 2 tablespoons butter or bacon drippings in skillet. Pour in egg mixture. Reduce heat; cook, lifting and folding occasionally, till eggs are set, but moist.

Pile eggs over deviled ham. Top with 4 tomato slices; place one half slice of sharp process American cheese over each tomato slice. Place loaf on baking sheet; broil about 4 inches from heat just till cheese melts. Serves 4.

Pizza Pronto and **Dad's Denvers** star as the fastest meals you'll ever fix—delicious supersized, multi-serving sandwiches to match the easy-going tempo of Saturdays or vacation time. Deck an informal table with these hearty sandwiches and let the family serve themselves. Great for casual evening entertaining too! Offer crisp relishes and potato chips as meal accompaniments and fresh fruit plate for dessert.

HOT HAM BUNS

¼ cup butter or margarine, softened
2 tablespoons prepared horseradish-mustard
2 teaspoons poppy seed
2 tablespoons finely chopped onion
4 hamburger buns, split
4 thin slices boiled ham
4 slices process Swiss cheese

Mix butter, mustard, poppy seed, and onion; spread on cut surfaces of buns. Tuck a slice of ham and cheese in each bun. Arrange on baking sheet. Bake in moderate oven (350°) about 20 minutes or till hot through. Makes 4.

MEAT-CHEESE OPEN FACERS

Combine 1 cup shredded sharp process cheese, 3 tablespoons mayonnaise, and 2 tablespoons chopped green onion. Slice one 12-ounce can luncheon meat in 12 thin slices. Lightly spread 6 slices toasted bread with prepared mustard; top each with 2 slices of meat. Top with cheese mixture. Broil 4 inches from heat 3 minutes or till melted. Makes 6.

CHICKEN CHEESE PUFF

1½ cups chopped cooked chicken
1 hard-cooked egg, chopped
¾ cup finely chopped celery
¼ cup pickle relish
¼ cup mayonnaise
Salt to taste
½ pound sharp process American cheese, softened at room temperature
1 well beaten egg
2 tablespoons mayonnaise
1 tablespoon prepared mustard
12 slices buttered white bread

Combine first 6 ingredients. Combine cheese and egg; blend with rotary beater or electric mixer; add mayonnaise and mustard; blend. Spread chicken mixture on 6 slices of bread. Top with remaining bread. Toast in broiler till golden on one side; turn and pile cheese mixture on each. Broil 3 to 4 inches from heat 2 to 3 minutes, or till slightly browned. Makes 6.

Stack a hearty sandwich

Ten-in-one Sandwich Loaf offers 10 scrumptious sandwiches in a single compact package. Zesty salami snuggles in between bread slices smothered with spunky cheese spread. In the oven, the cheese cloak melts and toasts golden. Trim with olives and parsley.

TEN-IN-ONE SANDWICH LOAF

2 5-ounce jars cheese spread
¼ cup mayonnaise or salad dressing
1 teaspoon prepared mustard
1 teaspoon grated onion
⅔ cup chopped pitted ripe olives
1 unsliced sandwich loaf
20 thin slices large salami

Blend first 4 ingredients; stir in olives. Cut crusts from *top* and both sides of loaf. Make ½-inch slices, cutting to, *but not through*, bottom crust. Spread facing sides of first cut with cheese filling. Repeat with *every other* cut.

Insert 2 salami slices in each "cheese sandwich." Spread remaining cheese mixture atop loaf. Tie string around loaf; brush sides with melted butter. Bake at 350° for 25 to 30 minutes. To serve, snip string and cut through bottom crust in unfilled sections. Makes 10.

CHEESEBURGER TOWERS

2 pounds ground beef
¼ cup finely chopped onion
1 tablespoon prepared mustard
1 tablespoon Worcestershire sauce
1½ teaspoons prepared horseradish
Salt and pepper

. . .

6 slices process American cheese
6 hamburger buns, split and toasted

Combine meat, onion, and seasonings. Shape in 12 patties, about ½ inch thick. Cook in lightly greased skillet about 6 minutes, turning once.

With cooky cutter, cut a 2-inch round from center of each cheese slice. Place half the meat patties in toasted buns; add cheese slice, filling the hole in cheese with catsup, mustard, or barbecue sauce; hamburger or hot-dog relish. Top with remaining meat patties, cheese rounds, and bun lids. Makes 6 sandwiches.

BLUE CHEESE TOPPER

Whip butter using electric mixer or rotary beater. Add crumbled blue cheese to taste. Spoon generous dollops on burgers just before whisking from broiler to toasted buns.

TORPEDOES

Brown individual (miniature) brown-and-serve French loaves according to the package directions. Split loaves in half, but don't cut quite through. (If you like, scoop out some of centers to make room for plenty of filling.) Spread with mustard, garlic butter, and/or mayonnaise with curry powder. (Or sprinkle bread with clear French or Italian dressing and dash with oregano, basil, or other herb.)

Line bottom halves with leaf lettuce. Pile on slices of corned beef, boiled ham, Bologna, salami, pickled tongue, chicken, tuna, herring —it's your choice of several or all. Add slices of American and Swiss cheese, onion rounds, green and ripe olive slices, sweet pickles—you name it. More lettuce, too. Anchor with cocktail picks. Each loaf makes 1 sandwich.

DOUBLE-BEEF SANDWICHES

12 slices rye bread, buttered
2 tablespoons prepared mustard
Leaf lettuce
4 ounces dried beef, pulled apart
4 ounces sliced Muenster or brick cheese
4 ounces cooked or canned corned beef, sliced very thin
2 large dill pickles, thinly sliced
1 onion, thinly sliced
1 tablespoon prepared horseradish

Spread *half* the bread slices with mustard; add layers of lettuce, dried beef, cheese, corned beef, pickle, and onion. Top each stack-up with more lettuce. Spread remaining bread slices with horseradish, and complete sandwiches. Anchor with toothpicks. Makes 6 sandwiches.

MARSHALL FIELD'S SPECIAL

For each serving, butter a large slice of rye bread. Place buttered side up; top with lettuce leaves and thin slices of Swiss cheese. Add a lettuce cup, reverse side up, and slices of white meat of chicken. Pour Thousand Island Dressing over. Top with slices of tomato and hard-cooked egg. Trim with crisp bacon.

ANTIPASTO SANDWICH

Cut a round loaf of bread *crosswise* into fourths. Before filling *each* layer, sprinkle the bread with wine vinegar, olive oil, and oregano. Place Bologna slices, canned pimiento and green peppers, and chicory on bottom later.

Top with second slice of bread. Layer with shredded lettuce, sliced tomatoes, hard-cooked egg slices, and anchovies.

Top with a third piece of bread. Layer with hard salami, Provolone cheese, and thin onion slices. Add remaining bread slice atop. Skewer sandwich to hold together. Garnish with parsley fluffs. Cut in wedges to serve 4.

This Antipasto Sandwich variation was concocted by a restaurant in New York City. A large round loaf of bread is split in fourths, then layered with the usual ingredients found on an antipasto tray. A wedge-shaped quarter of the gigantic sandwich is served to hungry customers.

Party-going sandwich fancies

CHUTNEY-CHEESE ROUNDS

1 3-ounce package cream cheese,
    softened
½ cup shredded sharp natural
    Cheddar cheese
1 teaspoon finely chopped onion
Dash Worcestershire sauce

    • • •

1½ dozen 2-inch white bread rounds
¼ cup chopped chutney

Combine cream cheese, shredded Cheddar cheese, onion, and Worcestershire sauce; beat with electric mixer or rotary beater till light and fluffy. Spread mixture on bread rounds and top each with a small amount of chutney. Chill until serving time. Makes 1½ dozen.

DATE-ROLL SANDWICHES

Soften one 3-ounce package cream cheese. Stir in 1 tablespoon milk and 2 tablespoons very finely chopped candied ginger. Slice canned date-nut roll ⅜ inch thick. Spread half the slices with cheese mixture. Top cheese with remaining slices. With a cooky cutter cut a crescent from side of each sandwich. Center piece makes a petal-shaped sandwich.

PARTY SANDWICH FILLING

1 8-ounce package cream cheese,
    softened
¾ cup chopped California walnuts
¼ cup chopped green pepper
¼ cup chopped onion
3 tablespoons chopped canned pimiento
1 tablespoon catsup
3 hard-cooked eggs, finely chopped
¾ teaspoon salt
Dash pepper

Combine all ingredients. Use as filling between lightly buttered slices of sandwich bread. Trim crusts. Cut each sandwich diagonally in 4 triangles. Makes 2⅓ cups filling.

FROSTED RIBBON LOAF

Ham Filling:
    1 cup ground cooked ham
    ⅓ cup finely chopped celery
    2 tablespoons drained pickle relish
    ½ teaspoon horseradish
    ¼ cup mayonnaise or salad dressing
Egg Filling:
    4 hard-cooked eggs, chopped
    ⅓ cup chopped stuffed green olives
    2 tablespoons minced green onions
    2 teaspoons prepared mustard
    ¼ cup mayonnaise or salad dressing
Unsliced sandwich loaf
4 3-ounce packages cream cheese,
    softened
⅓ cup milk

For Ham Filling combine first 5 ingredients. For Egg Filling combine next 5 ingredients. Slice bread lengthwise in 3 layers; trim crusts; butter slices. Spread first slice, buttered side up, with ham filling, second with egg filling; end with third slice. Wrap in foil; chill.

At serving time*, beat cream cheese with milk till fluffy. Frost top and sides of loaf. Sprinkle with snipped parsley. Makes 10 slices.

*Or, frost early; cover loosely; refrigerate.

SHRIMP TRIANGLES

1 3-ounce package cream cheese,
    softened
2 tablespoons mayonnaise
1 tablespoon catsup
1 teaspoon prepared mustard
Dash garlic powder
1 cup chopped canned shrimp
¼ cup finely chopped celery
1 teaspoon finely chopped onion
10 slices buttered sandwich bread

Blend cheese with mayonnaise; mix in catsup, mustard, and garlic powder. Stir in shrimp, celery, and onion. Use as a filling between slices of sandwich bread with crusts trimmed. Cut each sandwich in 4 triangles. Makes 20.

DEVILED HAM PINWHEELS

1 8-ounce package cream cheese,
  softened
1 4½-ounce can deviled ham
1 tablespoon catsup
1 to 2 teaspoons finely chopped onion
2 tablespoons chopped stuffed green
  olives
Unsliced sandwich loaf

Combine cheese, ham, catsup, onion, and
olives; beat with electric mixer or rotary beater.
Slice bread lengthwise in 7 slices. Remove
crusts. Spread about ¼ cup of ham filling on
each long slice of bread.

Roll up each slice starting from the narrow
end. Wrap in foil and chill thoroughly. Slice
each roll in 6 to 8 slices. Makes about 42.

WATER CRESS PINWHEELS

Combine 1 cup chopped water cress, two 3-
ounce packages cream cheese, softened, and
dash salt. Slice one unsliced sandwich loaf
lengthwise in ⅜-inch thick slices.

Remove crusts. Spread ¼ cup filling on each
slice. Roll up, starting at narrow end. Wrap in
foil and chill thoroughly. Slice ⅜-inch thick.
Makes about 2 dozen sandwiches.

JIGSAW SANDWICHES

1 3-ounce package cream cheese
1 tablespoon milk
1 teaspoon Worcestershire sauce
4 to 5 slices crisp-cooked bacon,
  crumbled
Sliced sandwich loaf
Sliced whole-wheat sandwich loaf

Soften cream cheese and blend in milk and
Worcestershire. Add bacon. Cut breads in 2-
inch rounds with cooky cutter. Spread *half* of
rounds (equal number white and whole-wheat
bread) with cheese mixture.

Divide the remaining rounds in three groups,
each with an equal number of light and dark
rounds to make Double Rounds, Stripes, and
Checkerboards as toppers for cheese rounds.

Double Rounds: With hole of doughnut cutter, cut tiny circles from center of rounds. Fit
the tiny whole-wheat circles in the holes of
large white ones and vice versa.

Stripes: Cut rounds in three strips, making
center strip widest. Fit together, alternating
white and whole-wheat strips; hold together
with bits of filling.

Checkerboards: Cut rounds in fourths. Make
checkerboards of white and whole wheat;
spread some cheese on edges to hold together.

Note: Freeze bread first; cut while frozen.

Pretty pinwheels filled
with creamy deviled ham
and crunchy water cress
surround a bowlful of dip
and assorted crackers—
holiday fare for elegant
open house entertaining.

SALADS AND VEGETABLES

Delightful is the word for salads that include cheese, whether they are "toss at the table" variety, or make-ahead molds. At family mealtime or when guests come, serve an enticing salad from this chapter. Some will accent a main dish. Others are a light meal in themselves. With fruit or vegetables, the added cheese is good insurance for smooth texture. Nippy cheeses such as blue and Cheddar do double duty with bold flavors.

Cheese-laced vegetables take on fascinating character. For many vegetables, a creamy cheese sauce is the perfect flavor companion. Shredded and tossed in a stuffing for tomatoes or squash, or just sprinkled atop a vegetable casserole, cheese adds hearty golden goodness.

Frosted Cheese Mold is the beauty pictured here. This chilly salad, made with both cottage and blue cheese, is flavor-sparked with limeade concentrate. It tastes cool enough to cheat the thermometer on warm summer days, but rich enough to let you know you're getting something substantial. Melon balls, orange sections, and frosted green grapes are the meant-to-be-eaten garnish for this frigid ring.

Superlative salads

FROSTED CHEESE MOLD

1 cup milk
2 envelopes (2 tablespoons) unflavored
  gelatin
2 12-ounce cartons (3 cups)
  cream-style cottage cheese
½ cup crumbled blue cheese
1 6-ounce can frozen limeade
  concentrate, thawed
½ cup broken pecans, toasted and
  salted
6 drops green food coloring
1 cup whipping cream, whipped

Pour milk into large saucepan. Sprinkle gelatin over milk to soften. Place over low heat and stir till gelatin is dissolved. Remove from heat.

Beat cottage and blue cheeses together till well blended; stir into gelatin mixture. Add concentrate, pecans, and food coloring. Fold in whipped cream. Turn into 6-cup ring mold and chill 4 to 6 hours. Unmold on serving plate; fill center with melon balls and orange sections. Garnish with frosted grapes and mint sprigs. Pass lime wedges. Makes 10 to 12 servings.

Note: To frost grapes, brush with slightly beaten egg white. Sprinkle with sugar.

FROZEN ORANGE MOLDS

1 8-ounce package cream cheese,
  softened
¼ cup orange juice
½ cup chopped pecans
1 8¾-ounce can (1 cup) crushed
  pineapple, drained
½ cup pitted dates, cut up
¼ cup chopped maraschino cherries
½ teaspoon grated orange peel
1 cup whipping cream, whipped

Combine cheese and orange juice, beating till fluffy. Stir in pecans and fruits. Fold in whipped cream. *Pack* into individual molds or into 8½x4½x2½-inch loaf pan. Freeze firm; let stand at room temperature about 15 minutes before serving. Makes 8 servings.

PEACH MELBA MOLD

1 1-pound can (2 cups) sliced peaches
2 tablespoons lemon juice
1 3-ounce package lemon-flavored
  gelatin
2 teaspoons milk
2 tablespoons mayonnaise or salad
  dressing
1 3-ounce package cream cheese,
  softened
2 tablespoons finely chopped pecans
1 10-ounce package frozen red
  raspberries, thawed
2 tablespoons lemon juice
1 3-ounce package raspberry-
  flavored gelatin

Peach layer: Drain peaches, reserving syrup. Combine syrup and 2 tablespoons lemon juice; add cold water to make 1 cup. Dissolve lemon gelatin in 1 cup *hot* water; add syrup mixture. Chill till partially set. Add peaches. Pour into 6½-cup ring mold. Chill till almost set.

Spread with *Cheese layer:* Mix milk, mayonnaise, and cream cheese; stir in pecans.

Raspberry layer: Drain raspberries, reserving syrup. Combine syrup and lemon juice; add cold water to make 1 cup. Dissolve raspberry gelatin in 1 cup *hot* water; add syrup mixture. Chill till partially set; stir in raspberries. Pour over cheese. Chill till firm. Unmold. Serves 8.

STRAWBERRY CREAM FREEZE

Pink and pretty with refreshing fruit flavor—

Combine one 8¾-ounce can (1 cup) crushed pineapple, drained, 1 cup strawberries, crushed, and ⅓ cup sugar; mix well.

Combine one 8-ounce carton (1 cup) cream-style cottage cheese and 2 teaspoons lemon juice; beat smooth with rotary or electric beater. Fold in ½ cup whipping cream, whipped, and fruit mixture. Turn into a 1-quart refrigerator tray; freeze firm, about 2 hours.

To serve, let stand at room temperature for 15 minutes. Cut in squares. Serves 5 or 6.

GREENGAGE PLUM SQUARES

1 1-pound 14-ounce can (3½ cups)
   greengage plums
1 3-ounce package lemon-flavored
   gelatin
1 3-ounce package lime-flavored gelatin
1 cup finely chopped celery
1 3-ounce package cream cheese,
   softened
3 tablespoons light cream
1 tablespoon mayonnaise

Drain plums, reserving syrup; pit and sieve plums. Add water to syrup to make 3½ cups; heat to boiling. Remove from heat. Add gelatin; stir to dissolve; add sieved plums. Chill till partially set; add celery. Turn into 8x8x2-inch pan. Blend last 3 ingredients. Spoon atop salad; swirl to marble. Chill till firm. Serves 9 to 12.

AVOCADO FRUIT SQUARES

1 large ripe avocado
2 tablespoons lemon juice
1 3-ounce package cream cheese,
   softened
2 tablespoons sugar
¼ cup mayonnaise or salad dressing
¼ teaspoon salt
1 cup well-drained diced canned
   peaches
¼ cup well-drained chopped
   maraschino cherries
½ cup whipping cream, whipped

Halve and seed avocado. Peel; dice into bowl. Sprinkle with 1 *tablespoon* of the lemon juice. Blend remaining lemon juice with next 4 ingredients. Add fruits; fold in whipped cream. Freeze in refrigerator tray 6 hours. Before serving, let stand at room temperature about 15 minutes; cut in squares. Serves 5 or 6.

BLUE CHEESE WALDORF SALAD

Combine 2 cups diced unpared tart apples, 1 cup diced celery, and ½ cup broken California walnuts. Mix ¼ cup crumbled blue cheese, ¼ cup dairy sour cream, ¼ cup mayonnaise or salad dressing, and dash salt; add to apple mixture and toss. Chill. Serve on greens. Serves 6.

FROZEN COCKTAIL SLICES

Soften two 3-ounce packages cream cheese; blend with 1 cup mayonnaise. Stir in one 1-pound 14-ounce can (3½ cups) fruit cocktail, well drained, ½ cup drained maraschino cherries, quartered, and 2½ cups tiny marshmallows (*or* 24 large marshmallows, cut up). Fold in 1 cup whipping cream, whipped. Tint with few drops red food coloring or maraschino-cherry juice, if desired. Pour into two 1-quart freezer containers. Freeze 6 hours or overnight. To serve, let stand out a few minutes, then remove from containers. Slice. Serves 10 to 12.

COOL-AS-A-CUCUMBER RING

1 envelope (1 tablespoon) unflavored
   gelatin
½ cup cold water
½ teaspoon salt
1½ cups shredded cucumber (about 2
   medium cucumbers)
2 12-ounce cartons (3 cups) cream-style
   cottage cheese
2 3-ounce packages cream cheese,
   softened
1 tablespoon shredded onion
½ cup mayonnaise or salad dressing
½ cup finely chopped celery

Soften gelatin in water; add salt. Heat and stir over low heat till gelatin dissolves. Halve cucumber and scrape out seeds; shred and drain before measuring. Beat cheeses together till blended. Stir in gelatin. Add cucumber and remaining ingredients. Pour into a 6½-cup ring mold. Chill till firm, 6 to 7 hours or overnight. Unmold. Makes 8 to 10 servings.

CARROT RELISH CUPS

Dissolve one 3-ounce package orange-flavored gelatin and ¼ cup sugar in 1½ cups boiling water. Add one 8-ounce package cream cheese, softened, and beat smooth with electric or rotary beater. Stir in ½ cup orange juice, ½ teaspoon grated lemon peel, and 2 tablespoons lemon juice. Chill till partially set. Add 1 cup shredded carrots and 1 cup chopped unpared apple. Spoon into 6 to 8 individual molds. Chill till firm. Unmold.

Salad Toss. Shred ½ large head lettuce in salad bowl. Over lettuce arrange row *each* of 4 cups diced cooked chicken; 2 medium tomatoes, diced; 3 hard-cooked eggs, chopped; 6 slices bacon, crisp-cooked and crumbled; and ¾ cup crumbled Roquefort cheese. Tuck in avocado wedges and endive leaves; sprinkle with cut chives. Toss at table; pass French dressing. Serves 4 to 6.

CHEF'S SALAD BOWL

Rub salad bowl with cut garlic clove. Tear 1 bunch leaf lettuce into bowl. Group atop: 2 cups cooked ham strips, 8 ounces sharp Cheddar cheese, cut in strips, and 3 hard-cooked eggs, sliced. Sprinkle with salt and pepper. Serve with favorite dressing. Serves 6.

STUFFED TOMATO FILLING

Combine 2 cups cream-style cottage cheese, 1 cup shredded sharp process American cheese, ½ cup sliced stuffed olives, and ¼ cup chopped walnuts. Fills 6 to 8 tomatoes.

HAM SALAD MOLD

Dissolve one 3-ounce package lemon-flavored gelatin in 1 cup hot water. Add ½ cup cold water, ½ cup mayonnaise, 1 teaspoon vinegar, 1 teaspoon prepared horseradish, ¾ teaspoon salt, and few drops bottled hot pepper sauce. Blend well with electric beater. Pour into refrigerator tray. Chill in freezing unit 15 to 20 minutes, till firm one inch from edge but soft in center. Turn into bowl; beat till fluffy. Fold in 1 cup diced, fully cooked ham, ½ cup shredded sharp process cheese, ¼ cup diced green pepper, 2 tablespoons diced pimiento, and 1 teaspoon grated onion. Pour into 1-quart mold. Chill firm, 30 to 60 minutes. Unmold. Serves 6.

CREAMY TUNA RING

½ envelope (1½ teaspoons) unflavored
   gelatin
1 12-ounce carton (1½ cups) cream-
   style cottage cheese
¼ cup chopped green pepper
2 tablespoons finely chopped green
   onions
¼ teaspoon salt
½ envelope (1½ teaspoons) unflavored
   gelatin
2 6½- or 7-ounce cans tuna, drained
   and flaked, or 1 1-pound can salmon,
   drained and flaked
½ cup chopped celery
¾ cup mayonnaise or salad dressing
2 tablespoons lemon juice

Soften 1½ teaspoons gelatin in 2 tablespoons
cold water; dissolve in ¼ cup hot water. Beat
cheese slightly; stir in dissolved gelatin, green
pepper, onions, and salt. Chill till partially set.
Pour into a 5-cup ring mold. Chill till almost
set. Meanwhile, soften the remaining gelatin
in 2 tablespoons cold water; dissolve *over* hot
water. Mix remaining ingredients; stir in gelatin. Chill till partially set. Spoon over cheese
layer. Chill till firm. Unmold. Serves 6.

CAULIFLOWER CHEESE TOSS

¼ cup olive oil
¼ cup salad oil
¼ cup white wine vinegar
1 teaspoon salt
Dash pepper
1 medium onion, thinly sliced and
   separated into rings
3 cups sliced fresh cauliflower
½ cup sliced radishes
Romaine leaves
1 medium head Iceberg lettuce, torn
   in bite-size pieces (about 8 cups)
2 ounces blue cheese, crumbled (½ cup)

Combine olive oil, salad oil, vinegar, salt, and
pepper. Add sliced vegetables to mixture. Mari-
nate for at least 30 minutes. Line salad bowl
with romaine leaves; add Iceberg lettuce;
sprinkle crumbled cheese over lettuce. Just before serving, add marinade mixture and toss
gently with lettuce and blue cheese. Serves 6.

COTTAGE POTATO SALAD

Chop 2 hard-cooked eggs; mix with 4 cups
cooked, cooled, sliced potatoes, 1 cup diced
celery, 1 cup large-curd cream-style cottage
cheese, ¾ cup mayonnaise or salad dressing,
½ cup sliced radishes, ½ cup diced green pepper, ¼ cup sliced green onions, 1 teaspoon salt,
and dash pepper. Chill. Garnish with hard-
cooked egg slices and ripe olives. Serves 6 to 8.

SKILLET HAM SALAD

¼ cup chopped green onions
¼ cup chopped green pepper
2 cups fully cooked ham, diced
1 tablespoon fat
3 or 4 medium potatoes, cooked, and
   diced (3 cups)
¼ teaspoon salt
Dash pepper
¼ cup mayonnaise or salad dressing
8 ounces sharp process American
   cheese, diced (1½ cups)

Cook onions, green pepper, and meat in hot
fat, stirring occasionally, till meat is lightly
browned. Add potatoes, salt, pepper, and mayonnaise. Heat, mixing lightly. Stir in cheese;
heat just till it begins to melt. Garnish with
green onions. Makes 4 servings.

MACARONI-AND-CHEESE SALAD

½ 7-ounce package (¾ cup) elbow
   macaroni, cooked, drained, and cooled
1 12-ounce can chopped ham, cut in
   strips
1 cup diced sharp natural Cheddar cheese
½ cup bias-cut celery slices
⅓ cup chopped green pepper
¼ cup sliced green onions and tops
2 tablespoons chopped canned
   pimiento
¼ cup drained pickle relish
½ cup mayonnaise or salad dressing
1 tablespoon prepared mustard
¼ teaspoon salt

Combine first 8 ingredients. Blend mayonnaise, mustard, and salt; add; toss lightly.
Chill. Serve on greens. Serves 6.

Creamy Blue Cheese Dressing. In mixing bowl, combine 1 cup crumbled blue cheese with 2 cups mayonnaise, ¼ cup vinegar, 2 table-spoons sugar, ½ cup dairy sour cream, and 1 clove garlic, minced. Beat with electric or rotary beater till fluffy. Chill. Makes 3½ cups.

FLUFFY ORANGE DRESSING

With electric beater, blend one 3-ounce package cream cheese, softened, 1 teaspoon grated orange peel, 2 tablespoons orange juice, 1 tablespoon lemon juice, 1 tablespoon honey, and ½ teaspoon salt.

Add ½ cup salad oil in a slow stream, beating constantly till dressing is fluffy. Chill. Stir dressing before serving. Serve over chilled fresh or canned fruit arranged in lettuce cups. Makes about 1 cup dressing.

LOW CALORIE HORSERADISH DRESSING

Place one 12-ounce carton (1½ cups) cream-style cottage cheese, 1 tablespoon milk, 1 tablespoon lemon juice, ½ teaspoon salt, and ¼ to ½ teaspoon prepared horseradish in a blender. Cover; blend at high speed till smooth.

Add 1 medium carrot, cut up, 3 radishes, halved, and 3 parsley sprigs. Turn blender on and off quickly just to chop vegetables. Chill till served. Makes 1¾ cups dressing.

Elegant vegetables

TOMATO CASSEROLE

1 medium onion, chopped
2 tablespoons butter or margarine
4 medium ripe tomatoes, sliced
4 ounces sharp process American cheese,
    shredded (1 cup)
1 cup fine soft bread crumbs
1 cup dairy sour cream
2 well beaten eggs
½ teaspoon salt

Cook onions in butter till tender. Place *half* the tomatoes in 10x6x1½-inch baking dish. Top with *half each* onions, cheese, and crumbs; repeat. Mix remaining ingredients. Pour over top; cover. Bake at 350° for 30 minutes. Uncover; bake 10 minutes longer. Makes 6 servings.

OLD-TIME STUFFED PEPPERS

For crisp pepper cups, don't precook peppers—

8 medium green peppers
1 pound ground beef
½ cup chopped onion
1½ cups fresh corn (3 to 4 ears) *or*
    1 12-ounce can whole-kernel corn,
    drained
1 8-ounce can tomato sauce
1 teaspoon Worcestershire sauce
¾ teaspoon salt
½ teaspoon monosodium glutamate
8 ounces sharp process American cheese,
    shredded (2 cups)
1 cup soft buttered bread crumbs

Cut off tops of green peppers; remove seeds and membranes. Precook pepper cups in boiling salted water about 5 minutes; drain. Sprinkle insides with salt.

Brown meat and onion; add next 5 ingredients; simmer till hot through, about 5 minutes. Add cheese and stir till melted. Stuff peppers; stand upright in 11x7x1½-inch baking dish. Sprinkle tops with crumbs. Fill baking dish to ½ inch with water. Bake uncovered at 350° for 40 minutes or till hot through. Serves 8.

POTATOES AU GRATIN

2 tablespoons butter or margarine
2 tablespoons all-purpose flour
¼ teaspoon salt
Dash white pepper
1 cup milk
4 ounces sharp process American
    cheese, shredded (1 cup)
4 cups hot sliced cooked potatoes
    (4 to 5 medium potatoes)
½ cup fine soft bread crumbs
1 tablespoon butter or margarine,
    melted

Melt 2 tablespoons butter in saucepan over low heat. Blend in flour, salt, and dash pepper. Add milk all at once. Cook quickly, stirring constantly, till mixture thickens and bubbles. Remove from heat.

Blend white sauce and cheese; combine with hot sliced potatoes. Pour into a 1-quart casserole. Toss crumbs with melted butter and sprinkle atop potatoes. Bake at 350° for 20 to 25 minutes or till browned. Serves 6 to 8.

ZUCCHINI BOATS

4 medium zucchini (2 pounds)
¼ pound bulk pork sausage
¼ cup chopped onion
½ cup fine cracker crumbs
1 slightly beaten egg
½ cup grated Parmesan cheese
½ teaspoon monosodium glutamate
¼ teaspoon salt
¼ teaspoon thyme
Dash *each* garlic salt and pepper

Cook whole zucchini in boiling salted water till barely tender, 7 to 10 minutes. Cut in half lengthwise; scoop squash from shells and mash. Cook sausage and onion; drain off excess fat. Stir in mashed zucchini. Reserve 2 tablespoons cheese; mix in remaining ingredients. Spoon into zucchini shells; place in shallow baking dish. Sprinkle with Parmesan. Bake at 350° for 25 to 30 minutes. Makes 4 servings.

CREAMY CORN

1 3-ounce package cream cheese,
  softened
1/4 cup milk
1 tablespoon butter or margarine
1/2 teaspoon onion salt
1 1-pound can (2 cups) whole kernel
  corn, drained

In a saucepan, combine the cream cheese, milk,
butter, and onion salt. Stir over low heat till
cheese melts. Add corn; heat through and serve.
Garnish with parsley or paprika. Serves 4 or 5.

CARROTS AU GRATIN

3 cups cooked sliced carrots, drained
1 10 1/2-ounce can condensed cream of
  celery soup
4 ounces process American cheese,
  shredded (1 cup)
1/4 cup fine dry bread crumbs
1 tablespoon melted butter or margarine

Combine carrots, soup, and cheese in a 1-quart
casserole. Combine bread crumbs and butter;
sprinkle atop carrot mixture. Bake at 350° for
20 to 25 minutes. Makes 4 servings.

ARTICHOKE VELVET

2 9-ounce packages frozen artichoke
  hearts
1 pint fresh mushrooms, sliced
2 tablespoons butter or margarine
One 1 1/16-ounce package chicken
  gravy mix
1 cup water
Dash *each* thyme and marjoram
4 ounces natural Swiss cheese,
  diced (1 cup)
1 tablespoon dry white wine

Cook artichokes according to package directions; drain. Cook mushrooms in butter till tender. Combine artichokes and mushrooms in 1-
quart casserole. Prepare chicken gravy mix using package directions. Remove from heat; add
herbs and cheese; stir till cheese melts. Add
wine; pour over vegetables. Bake covered at
350° for 30 minutes. Makes 6 to 8 servings.

COMPANY VEGETABLE BAKE

2 10-ounce packages frozen peas and
  carrots
1 9-ounce package frozen whole green
  beans
1 5-ounce can water chestnuts, drained
  and sliced
1 3-ounce can broiled sliced
  mushrooms, drained (1/2 cup)
    • • •
1 10 1/2-ounce can condensed cream of
  mushroom soup
3 to 4 tablespoons cooking sherry
1 teaspoon Worcestershire sauce
Dash bottled hot pepper sauce
8 ounces sharp process American
  cheese, shredded (2 cups)
    • • •
1/4 cup rich-round-cracker crumbs

Cook peas and carrots, and beans till just barely tender; drain. Combine with water chestnuts
and mushrooms. Combine remaining ingredients, except crumbs, for sauce; toss with vegetables. Turn into a 2-quart casserole.
  Bake uncovered at 350° for 40 to 45 minutes,
till hot and bubbly. Stir occasionally. Sprinkle
with crumbs before serving. Serves 10 to 12.

COMPANY CAULIFLOWER

1 medium head cauliflower
Salt
Pepper
1 cup dairy sour cream
4 ounces sharp process American
  cheese, shredded (1 cup)
2 teaspoons toasted sesame seed*

Rinse cauliflower; break into flowerets. Cook
covered in small amount boiling salted water
till tender, 10 to 15 minutes; drain *well*.
  Place *half* the cauliflower in a 1-quart casserole; season with salt and pepper. Spread with
1/2 cup sour cream; sprinkle with 1/2 *cup* cheese
and *1 teaspoon* sesame seed. Repeat layers.
  Bake in a moderate oven (350°) till cheese
melts and sour cream is heated through, about
5 minutes. Makes 6 servings.
  *To toast sesame seed, place in shallow pan
in a moderate oven (350°) for 10 minutes or till
browned, shaking occasionally.

DE LUXE LIMAS

    1 10-ounce package frozen green Limas
    1 11-ounce can condensed Cheddar
        cheese soup
    1/2 cup milk
    3/4 cup sliced celery
    1/4 cup snipped parsley
    1 3 1/2-ounce can French-fried onions

Empty frozen Limas into a bowl; pour boiling water over and break apart. Drain well.

Blend together soup and milk; add Limas, celery, and parsley. Stir in *half* the onions. Place mixture in a 1-quart casserole. Bake at 350° for 35 minutes. Border casserole with remaining onions. Bake 10 minutes longer or till onions are crisp. Makes 6 servings.

CHEESE STUFFED ONIONS

Peel 6 medium onions; cook in boiling salted water till just tender, about 25 minutes; drain and cool. Remove centers; chop 1/2 cup onion centers and combine with 3/4 cup cottage cheese, 2 tablespoons finely chopped green pepper, 6 slices crisp-cooked bacon, crumbled, 1/2 teaspoon garlic salt and dash salt.

Stuff onion shells and place in 1 1/2-quart casserole. Top with 1/2 cup buttered bread crumbs and 6 strips canned pimiento. Cover and bake in a moderate oven (350°) for 20 minutes; uncover and bake 10 minutes longer. Serves 6.

BLUE-CHEESED MUSHROOMS

    12 to 14 large fresh or canned whole
        mushrooms
    1/4 cup chopped green onions
    1/4 cup butter or margarine
            . . .
    1 ounce blue cheese, crumbled (1/4 cup)
    1/3 cup fine dry bread crumbs

Remove stems from mushrooms; chop stems. Cook stems and onions in butter till tender but not brown. Add cheese, 2 *tablespoons* of the crumbs, and salt and pepper to taste. Fill mushroom crowns with mixture; sprinkle with remaining crumbs. Place on baking sheet. Bake at 350° for 12 minutes for fresh mushrooms or 8 minutes for canned. Serves 4 to 6.

GREEN BEAN-CHEESE BAKE

    2 9-ounce packages frozen cut
        green beans
    1 8-ounce can (1 cup) small white
        onions, drained
    4 slices bacon
    1 tablespoon all-purpose flour
    1/2 cup tomato juice
    4 ounces sharp process American
        cheese, shredded (1 cup)
    1 tablespoon prepared mustard

Cook and drain beans, reserving 1/4 cup liquid. Arrange green beans and onions in 10x6x1 1/2-inch baking dish. Fry bacon; drain, reserving 1 tablespoon fat. Blend flour into fat; add tomato juice and bean liquid. Cook and stir till thick. Add cheese and mustard; stir till smooth. Pour over vegetables; stir lightly. Crumble bacon over top. Bake at 375° for 20 minutes. Makes 6 servings.

CHEESE BROILED EGGPLANT

    1 small eggplant
    2 tablespoons salad oil
    Mozzarella cheese slices

Cut eggplant into crosswise slices 1/4-inch thick; pare each slice. Place on broiler pan. Brush with salad oil; season to taste. Broil till light brown, about 5 minutes; turn; brush and season. Broil 3 minutes. Top with cheese; broil till cheese melts, about 2 minutes. Serves 4 to 6.

BROCCOLI CASSEROLE

    2 tablespoons butter, melted
    2 tablespoons all-purpose flour
    1 3-ounce package cream cheese,
        softened
    1 ounce blue cheese, crumbled (1/4 cup)
    1 cup milk
    2 10-ounce packages frozen chopped
        broccoli, cooked and drained
    1/3 cup rich round crackers, crushed

In a saucepan blend butter, flour, and cheeses. Add milk; cook and stir to boiling. Stir in broccoli. Place in 1-quart casserole; top with crumbs. Bake at 350° for 30 minutes. Serves 8.

SOUPS AND SAUCES

Here you'll find soups like Grandmother
used to make bubbling in a
gigantic kettle on her big wood stove.
The flavor's just as good
and the method's twice as easy!

In a toot? Count on some of the speedy
fix-ups using canned soups.
Cheese and seasonings team up for gusto!

Try hearty cheese soups for a quick
pick-me-up snack, nourishing meal,
or as a compatible sandwich partner.

Discover how subtle cheese sauces can
give an elegant lift to vegetables,
omelets, and meats. Such superb sauces
are a true gourmet's delight.

Canadian Cheese Soup and **Chicken-cheese Chowder** are perfect for a home-style supper, brunch, or any family get-together. Rich, creamy Canadian Cheese Soup, in the brass tureen, blends sharp cheese with vegetables. Chicken-cheese Chowder dresses up a canned soup—bits of bacon and tiny bites of chicken mingle with mild Monterey Jack cheese. Accompany these hearty soups with relishes, crackers, bread sticks, or toast rounds. For dessert, offer fresh fruit and cookies.

Soups: simply delicious

ONION AND CHEESE SOUP

- 3 tablespoons butter or margarine
- 1 cup chopped mild onions
- 3 tablespoons all-purpose flour
- ½ teaspoon salt
- Dash pepper
- 4 cups milk
- 8 ounces sharp process American cheese, shredded (2 cups)
- Toasted bread rounds, buttered and topped with Parmesan cheese

Melt butter; cook onion till tender but not brown. Blend in flour, salt, and pepper. Add milk all at once. Cook, stirring constantly, till mixture thickens and bubbles. Add cheese; stir to melt. Float toast rounds, garnished with olive slices, atop. Makes 6 to 8 servings.

CANADIAN CHEESE SOUP

- ½ cup finely chopped onion
- ¼ cup butter or margarine
- ½ cup all-purpose flour
- 4 cups milk
- 4 cups chicken broth
- ½ cup finely diced carrots
- ½ cup finely diced celery
- Dash *each* salt and paprika
- 1 cup diced sharp process American cheese

Cook onion in butter till tender but not brown. Blend in flour. Add milk, broth, carrots, celery, salt, and paprika. Cook and stir over medium heat till mixture thickens and bubbles. Reduce heat; add cheese; stir to melt. Simmer 15 minutes. Trim with popcorn. Serves 8.

Onion and Cheese Soup served piping hot will give a gourmet touch to any meal. Mild onions simmer in a creamy sauce delicately flavored with cheese. Toasty bread rounds topped with zippy Parmesan cheese and green olive slices make the garnish both tasty, attractive.

CHICKEN-CHEESE CHOWDER

4 slices bacon
¼ cup chopped onion
2 tablespoons chopped green pepper
2 cups milk
1 10½-ounce can condensed cream of chicken soup
1 cup diced cooked chicken
2 tablespoons chopped canned pimiento
Dash salt
4 ounces Monterey Jack cheese, shredded (1 cup)
Dash paprika *or* mace

Cook bacon till crisp; drain and crumble. Put 2 tablespoons drippings in saucepan. Add onion and green pepper; cook till tender. Add milk, soup, chicken, pimiento, salt, and half the bacon. Heat through. Add cheese; stir to melt. To serve, garnish with remaining bacon and paprika or mace. Makes 4 or 5 servings.

PACIFIC CHOWDER

Cook one 10-ounce package frozen baby Lima beans according to package directions for 20 minutes; do not drain. Stir in one 10½-ounce can condensed cream of chicken soup, one 1-pound can tomatoes, and one 6½- or 7-ounce can tuna, drained.

Cook over medium heat, stirring occasionally, till soup is hot. Add 1 cup shredded sharp process American cheese; stir till cheese melts. Makes 6 to 8 servings.

ALPINE POTATO SOUP

2 cups milk
1 10½-ounce can condensed cream of potato soup
1 cup cooked peas
½ teaspoon dry mustard
4 ounces natural Swiss cheese, shredded (1 cup)
4 slices bacon, crisp-cooked
Paprika

Combine milk, soup, peas, and mustard; heat. Add cheese; stir to melt. Top each serving with paprika and crumbled bacon. Serves 6.

CHEESY ASPARAGUS SOUP

2 tablespoons butter or margarine
2 tablespoons all-purpose flour
1 teaspoon salt
Dash nutmeg
Dash pepper
3 cups milk
1 10-ounce package frozen cut asparagus, cooked and drained
6 ounces natural Cheddar cheese, shredded (1½ cups)
Paprika
Grated Parmesan cheese

Melt butter and blend in flour, salt, nutmeg, and pepper. Add milk all at once. Cook, stirring constantly, till mixture thickens and bubbles. Cook 2 minutes longer. Add asparagus (cut any large pieces) and cheese; stir till cheese melts. Garnish with paprika and Parmesan cheese. Makes 6 servings.

QUICK VICHYSSOISE

1½ cups water
2 tablespoons snipped parsley
2 chicken bouillon cubes
1 cup light cream
Packaged instant mashed potatoes (enough for 4 servings)
1 4-ounce package whipped cream cheese with onion
Snipped chives

Combine water, parsley, and bouillon cubes; bring to boiling; stir to dissolve cubes. Remove from heat; add cream; stir in potatoes. Cool at room temperature 15 minutes. Add cheese; blend in blender till smooth. Chill. Garnish with chives. Makes 4 to 6 servings.

GOLDEN CHEESE SOUP

In saucepan, melt ¼ cup butter or margarine. Add ½ cup shredded carrots and ¼ cup chopped onion; cook till tender. Blend in ¼ cup all-purpose flour, dash salt, dash pepper.

Add 2½ cups milk all at once. Cook, stirring constantly, till thickened. Add 2 cups shredded natural Cheddar cheese; stir to melt. Blend in ½ cup ale or beer; heat. Makes 6 servings.

Subtle sauces

CHEDDAR CHEESE SAUCES

• Melt 2 tablespoons butter or margarine; blend in 2 tablespoons all-purpose flour and 1/4 teaspoon salt. Add 1 cup milk; cook, stirring constantly, till mixture thickens and bubbles. Add 1 cup shredded sharp natural Cheddar cheese. Stir till melted. Makes 1 1/2 cups sauce.
• Combine one can condensed cream of mushroom soup, 1/3 cup milk; heat. Add 1 cup shredded Cheddar cheese; stir to melt.
• Melt 2 cups shredded sharp process American cheese over hot water. Slowly stir in 1/2 cup milk. Stir frequently to blend.
• In top of double boiler, combine 1/2 cup mayonnaise or salad dressing, 1/4 cup shredded sharp process American cheese, and 1 tablespoon milk. Heat and stir over hot water till melted.

SWISS CHEESE SAUCE

2 ounces process Swiss cheese, shredded (1/2 cup)
1/4 cup mayonnaise or salad dressing
1/2 cup dairy sour cream

Combine cheese and mayonnaise. Cook over low heat, stirring constantly, till cheese melts. (If necessary, beat smooth with rotary beater.) Mix in sour cream; heat through. Dash with paprika. Serve with vegetables. Makes 1 cup.

SWISS-CHEDDAR SAUCE

2 tablespoons butter or margarine
2 tablespoons all-purpose flour
1/4 teaspoon salt
1 1/4 cups milk
2 ounces sharp process American cheese, shredded (1/2 cup)
2 ounces process Swiss cheese, shredded (1/2 cup)

Melt butter; blend in flour and salt. Add milk all at once. Cook, stirring constantly, till mixture thickens and bubbles. Remove from heat; stir in cheeses till melted. Makes 1 1/2 cups.

MORNAY SAUCE

2 tablespoons butter or margarine
2 tablespoons all-purpose flour
1/4 teaspoon salt
Dash white pepper
1 1/2 cups milk
1/2 cup diced Gruyere cheese

Melt butter; blend in flour, salt, and pepper. Add milk all at once. Cook quickly, stirring constantly, till mixture thickens and bubbles. Add cheese; stir till melted. Serve over vegetables, omelets, or souffles. Makes 1 3/4 cups.

PARMESAN SAUCE IMPERIAL

1 tablespoon butter or margarine
1 tablespoon all-purpose flour
1/4 teaspoon salt
Dash pepper
Dash paprika
Dash dry mustard
1 cup milk
2 tablespoons grated Parmesan cheese
2 tablespoons toasted slivered almonds

Melt butter; blend in flour and seasonings. Add milk all at once. Cook, stirring constantly till mixture thickens and bubbles. Add cheese and almonds; stir till cheese melts. Serve with vegetables, omelets. Makes 1 cup.

ZIPPY BLUE CHEESE SAUCE

2 tablespoons butter or margarine
2 tablespoons all-purpose flour
1 cup milk
1 chicken bouillon cube
1/4 cup dairy sour cream
1/4 cup crumbled blue cheese

Melt butter; blend in flour. Add milk and bouillon cube. Cook and stir till mixture thickens and bubbles. Remove from heat; stir in sour cream and cheese. Heat through; do not boil. Serve with vegetables. Makes 1 1/4 cups.

CHEF'S CHEESE SAUCE

4 ounces sharp process American cheese,
  shredded (1 cup)
¼ cup butter or margarine, softened
½ cup dairy sour cream
2 tablespoons chopped green onions

With electric mixer or rotary beater, whip
cheese and butter till light and fluffy. Whip in
sour cream and onions till blended. Serve with
baked potatoes. Makes 1⅓ cups sauce.

SHRIMP ALMOND SAUCE

¼ cup chive cream cheese
¼ cup milk
1 10-ounce can frozen condensed cream
  of shrimp soup
2 teaspoons lemon juice
2 tablespoons toasted sliced almonds

In saucepan, blend cheese and milk. Add soup;
heat and stir till hot. Add lemon juice. Pour
over hot cooked vegetables. Sprinkle with almonds. Makes 1½ cups sauce.

HORSERADISH SAUCE

1 8-ounce package cream cheese
1 tablespoon sugar
2 to 3 tablespoons prepared horseradish
1 tablespoon lemon juice
1 teaspoon Worcestershire sauce
½ cup whipping cream, whipped

Soften cream cheese; blend in sugar, horseradish, lemon juice, and Worcestershire. Fold
in whippped cream. Pass with ham, corned beef,
or cold cuts. Makes 2 cups sauce.

CARAWAY CHEESE SAUCE

1 11-ounce can condensed Cheddar
  cheese soup
1 cup dairy sour cream
1 teaspoon caraway seeds, crushed
¼ teaspoon aromatic bitters

Combine all ingredients in saucepan. Heat
through, but do not boil. Serve with baked potatoes or vegetables. Makes 2 cups.

MOCK HOLLANDAISE SAUCE

1 3-ounce package cream cheese,
  softened
2 tablespoons milk
1 egg yolk
1½ teaspoons lemon juice
Dash salt

Blend cream cheese and milk. Add egg yolk and
blend thoroughly. Add lemon juice and salt;
beat well. Cook over low heat, stirring constantly, till of a nice sauce consistency. Serve
over vegetables. Makes about ½ cup.

CHIVE SAUCE

1 4-ounce carton chive whipped
  cream cheese
¼ cup milk
¼ teaspoon salt

Blend whipped cream cheese with milk. Heat
and stir over low heat just till warm. Combine
hot cooked new potatoes and peas in serving
dish; pour cream-cheese sauce over.

SHRIMP CHEESE SAUCE

Melt 2 tablespoons butter; blend in 2 tablespoons flour. Stir in one 10-ounce can frozen
condensed cream of shrimp soup and 1 soup can
milk. Cook and stir till sauce thickens. Add ½
cup shredded sharp process American cheese;
stir till melted. Serve with egg dishes.

CHEESY EGG SAUCE

1 cup chopped celery
¼ cup chopped green pepper
¼ cup finely chopped onion
1 10½-ounce can condensed cream of
  celery soup
½ cup milk
1 cup diced process American cheese
4 hard-cooked eggs, chopped
6 stuffed green olives, sliced

Cook vegetables in 2 tablespoons hot fat till
tender. Add soup, milk, and cheese; heat and
stir till cheese melts. Add chopped eggs and
olives; heat. Serve on toast points. Serves 4.

DESSERTS

Savor the many delicious desserts that start off with cheese. Cheesecake may be the first to come to mind because of its rich moist texture and the endless flavor variations. Many other dessert ideas begin with cheese—individual tarts, creamy pies, crisp cookies, smooth ice creams, and even frostings. Mild cheeses such as cream and cottage, are carriers for other wonderful dessert flavors. Other cheeses stand on their own flavor merits.

For elegant simplicity, colorful cheese and fruit trays are real spectaculars. They're a snap to arrange, and just right for that delicate mealtime finale. A popular variant on this idea is a fruit pie, especially apple, topped with a sharp cheese, especially Cheddar.

Remember when you're serving dessert cheeses, that most cheeses reveal their truest flavors when they're eaten at room temperature.

Angel Cheesecake, a dessert conversation piece to climax your next late-evening supper. Tangy yet mellow, it tastes like cheesecake, but it has the light texture of angel cake. Give it a glamorous setting. Rose-shaped candlesticks holding long graceful tapers, and tinted sugar cubes, coordinate with your tablecloth.

ANGEL CHEESECAKE

It tastes like cheesecake, but its texture is light—like an angel cake—

Crust:
1 cup (9 slices) zwieback crumbs
2 tablespoons sugar
2 tablespoons butter or margarine, melted

Filling:
½ cup sugar
2 8-ounce packages cream cheese, softened
1 teaspoon vanilla
¼ teaspoon salt
½ teaspoon grated lemon peel
2 cups dairy sour cream
5 egg yolks

• • •

5 egg whites
1 tablespoon lemon juice
½ cup sugar

Cherry Sauce:
½ cup sugar
2 tablespoons cornstarch
Dash salt
1 1-pound 4-ounce can frozen, pitted, tart red cherries (with syrup), thawed

Crust: Mix zwieback crumbs, 2 tablespoons sugar, and the butter or margarine; press on bottom of ungreased 9-inch spring-form pan.

Filling: Gradually beat ½ cup sugar into softened cream cheese. Beat in vanilla, ¼ teaspoon salt, and grated lemon peel. Add sour cream and blend in egg yolks.

Beat egg whites with lemon juice to soft peaks; gradually add ½ cup sugar, beating till *very stiff*, but not dry, peaks form. Fold the cheese mixture into egg whites. Gently pour into crumb-lined pan. Bake in slow oven (325°) for 1¼ hours or till knife inserted halfway between center and edge comes out clean.

Cool 10 minutes; run spatula around edge of top. (Cake settles slightly as it cools—loosening edge lets it do this evenly.) Cool thoroughly, about 1½ hours, before removing sides of pan. Chill thoroughly.

Pass *Cherry Sauce:* In saucepan, combine sugar, cornstarch, and salt. Stir in thawed cherries. Cook and stir over medium heat till mixture thickens and comes to boiling. Reduce heat; simmer 10 minutes. Chill before serving.

CAFE AU LAIT CHEESECAKE

¾ cup sugar
2 envelopes (2 tablespoons) unflavored gelatin
¼ teaspoon salt
2 beaten egg yolks
1 cup milk
2 tablespoons instant coffee powder
2 12-ounce cartons (3 cups) cream-style cottage cheese, undrained and sieved
1 teaspoon vanilla
2 egg whites
¼ cup sugar
1 cup whipping cream, whipped
½ cup graham-cracker crumbs (7 crackers)
1 tablespoon sugar
2 tablespoons butter or margarine, melted

Blend sugar, gelatin, and salt. Stir in egg yolks and milk. Cook and stir over low heat till gelatin dissolves. Blend in coffee powder; cool. Stir in cottage cheese and vanilla. Chill, stirring occasionally, till mixture mounds when spooned. Beat egg whites to soft peaks; gradually add ¼ cup sugar, beating to stiff peaks. Fold into gelatin mixture; then fold in whipped cream. Pour into 8- or 9-inch spring-form pan. Combine remaining ingredients; sprinkle over cake; chill 3 to 4 hours before serving.

MARBLE CHEESECAKE

Combine one 12-ounce box vanilla wafers, crushed (2½ cups), and ½ cup butter or margarine, melted; press on bottom and sides of a 9-inch spring-form pan or 13x9x2-inch baking pan. Chill. Combine ½ cup sugar and 1 envelope (1 tablespoon) unflavored gelatin; stir in 1 cup milk. Heat and stir till sugar and gelatin dissolve. Cool till mixture begins to thicken.

Beat together one 8-ounce package cream cheese, softened, ½ cup sugar and 1½ teaspoons vanilla; blend in gelatin mixture. Beat one 14-ounce can (1⅔ cups) evaporated milk, *chilled icy cold,* to stiff peaks; fold into cheese. Place ⅓ of mixture in small bowl. Sift ¼ cup cocoa over; gently fold in. Alternately spoon vanilla and chocolate mixtures into crust; swirl. Chill 8 hours. Serves 8 to 10.

HONEY-RAISIN CHEESECAKE

1 cup sifted all-purpose flour
¼ cup sugar
¼ teaspoon salt
¼ cup butter or margarine
1 slightly beaten egg
½ cup light raisins
2 12-ounce cartons (3 cups) cream-style
   cottage cheese
4 eggs
½ cup honey
¼ cup sifted all-purpose flour
¼ cup sugar
1 teaspoon grated lemon peel
½ teaspoon vanilla
¼ teaspoon salt
¼ cup toasted sliced almonds

Mix 1 cup flour, ¼ cup sugar and ¼ teaspoon salt; cut in butter till mixture resembles coarse crumbs. Blend in beaten egg. Pat dough evenly on bottom and 1 inch up sides of an 8x8x2-inch baking dish. Bake in a hot oven (400°) for 15 minutes; cool. Sprinkle raisins over crust.

Beat cottage cheese with electric or rotary beater till smooth. Add 4 eggs, one at a time, beating well after each addition. Add honey, ¼ cup flour, ¼ cup sugar, lemon peel, vanilla, and ¼ teaspoon salt; blend well. Pour mixture over raisins. Sprinkle top with toasted almonds. Bake in a slow oven (325°) for 40 minutes or till set. Cut in 9 or 12 squares.

PUDDING 'N PINEAPPLE CAKE

Graham Crust: Combine 1¼ cups fine graham-cracker crumbs, 2 tablespoons sugar, and ⅓ cup melted butter; press onto bottom and sides of 11x7x1½-inch baking dish.

Pineapple Filling: Drain 1½ cups cream-style cottage cheese, reserving liquid; add milk to liquid to measure 2¼ cups. Beat cheese till fluffy. In saucepan, mix 1 package lemon pudding-and-pie filling and 1 tablespoon unflavored gelatin. Prepare according to *label directions for pie filling*, using 2¼ cups milk instead of water. Stir in one 8¾-ounce can crushed pineapple (with syrup) and cheese. Beat 2 egg whites to soft peaks. Gradually add ¼ cup sugar; beat to stiff peaks; fold into gelatin.

Pour mixture into crust. Chill till set. Cut in 10 or 12 squares; trim with strawberries.

PETITE CHERRY CHEESECAKES

Beat together two 8-ounce packages cream cheese, softened, ¾ cup sugar, 2 eggs, 1 tablespoon lemon juice, and 1 teaspoon vanilla till light and fluffy. Line small muffin pans with 24 paper bake cups; place a vanilla wafer in bottom of each. Fill cups ⅔ full with cheese mixture. Bake at 375° for 15 to 20 minutes or just till set. Top each with about 1 tablespoon cherry pie filling (takes one 1-pound 5-ounce can); chill. Makes 2 dozen cakes.

SURPRISE CHEESECAKE

Real honest-to-goodness cheesecake that can go on the weight-watcher's list!—

2 tablespoons unflavored gelatin
½ cup sugar
¼ teaspoon salt
2 egg yolks
1 cup reliquefied nonfat dry milk*
   or skim milk
1 teaspoon grated lemon peel
2 12-ounce cartons (3 cups) cream-style
   cottage cheese, undrained and sieved
1 tablespoon lemon juice
1 teaspoon vanilla
2 egg whites
¼ cup sugar
½ cup nonfat dry milk
½ cup ice water
⅓ cup fine graham-cracker crumbs
Dash cinnamon
Dash nutmeg

Thoroughly mix gelatin, ½ cup sugar, and salt. Beat together egg yolks and milk; add to gelatin mixture and cook over low heat, stirring constantly, just until gelatin is dissolved. Remove from heat; add lemon peel; cool. Stir in cottage cheese, lemon juice, and vanilla. Chill, stirring occasionally, till mixture mounds. Beat egg whites till soft peaks form; gradually add ¼ cup sugar and beat to stiff peaks. Combine dry milk and ice water; whip till stiff peaks form. Fold egg whites and whipped milk into gelatin mixture. Combine cracker crumbs and spices. Sprinkle half over bottom of 8-inch spring-form pan. Pour in cheese mixture. Top with remaining crumbs. Chill till firm. Serves 12.

*Follow package directions.

Press crust mixture on bottom and sides of a 9-inch spring-form pan with fingers. Make sides about 1¾ inches high, tilting pan for ease.

CHEESECAKE SUPREME

Crust:
  1 cup sifted all-purpose flour
  ¼ cup sugar
  1 teaspoon grated lemon peel
  ½ cup butter or margarine
  1 slightly beaten egg yolk
  ¼ teaspoon vanilla

Filling:
  5 8-ounce packages cream cheese,
    softened
  ¼ teaspoon vanilla
  ¾ teaspoon grated lemon peel
  1¾ cups sugar
  3 tablespoons all-purpose flour
  4 or 5 eggs (1 cup)
  2 egg yolks
  ¼ cup whipping cream

Crust: Mix first 3 ingredients. Cut in butter till crumbly. Add yolk and vanilla; mix. Pat ⅓ of dough on bottom of 9-inch spring-form pan (sides removed). Bake at 400° for 8 minutes; cool. Butter sides; attach to bottom; pat remaining dough on sides 1¾ inches high.

Filling: Beat cheese; add vanilla and peel. Mix sugar, flour, and ¼ teaspoon salt; slowly add to cheese. Add eggs and yolks one at a time, beating after each. Gently add cream. Turn into pan. Bake at 450° for 12 minutes; reduce heat to 300°; bake 55 minutes or till knife inserted off-center comes out clean. Cool ½ hour; loosen cake from sides. Cool ½ hour; remove pan sides. Cool 2 hours; chill. Serves 12.

STRAWBERRY-GLAZED CHEESECAKE

Always welcome. Come summer, top with a fresh raspberry or blueberry glaze—

Crust:
  1¾ cups fine graham-cracker crumbs
    (about 20 crackers)
  ¼ cup finely chopped walnuts
  ½ teaspoon cinnamon
  ½ cup butter or margarine, melted

Filling:
  3 well beaten eggs
  2 8-ounce packages cream cheese,
    softened
  1 cup sugar
  ¼ teaspoon salt
  2 teaspoons vanilla
  ½ teaspoon almond extract
  3 cups dairy sour cream

Glaze:
  1 pint fresh strawberries
  ¾ cup water
  2 tablespoons cornstarch
  ½ cup sugar
  Red food coloring

Thoroughly mix ingredients for crust. Press on bottom and sides of 9-inch spring-form pan. Sides should be about 1¾ inches high.

Combine eggs, cream cheese, sugar, salt, vanilla, and almond extract; beat till smooth. Blend in sour cream. Pour into crumb crust. Bake in a moderate oven (375°) about 35 minutes or just till set. Cool. Chill thoroughly, about 4 to 5 hours. (Filling will be soft.)

For glaze: Crush 1 *cup* of the strawberries; add water and cook 2 minutes; sieve. Mix cornstarch with sugar; slowly stir in hot berry mixture. Bring to boiling, stirring constantly. Cook and stir till mixture is thick and clear. (Add a few drops red food coloring if desired.) Cool to room temperature. Place remaining strawberries atop chilled cheesecake; pour glaze over. Chill about 2 hours. Makes 10 servings.

Strawberry-Glazed Cheesecake—a real "dazzler." Velvety filling in a crisp crust. The glaze? Made with fresh strawberries, of course.

FRENCH STRAWBERRY TART

2 8-ounce packages cream cheese,
    softened
1/4 cup sugar
1 to 2 teaspoons grated lemon peel
2 tablespoons lemon juice
1 10-inch baked pastry shell
1 quart fresh strawberries, sliced
2 tablespoons cornstarch
1/4 cup cold water
1 12-ounce jar (1 cup) strawberry
    preserves
2 tablespoons lemon juice

Combine cheese, sugar, lemon peel, and 2 table-spoons lemon juice; mix well. Spread in bottom of baked shell. Top with strawberries. Combine cornstarch and water; add preserves. Bring to boiling, stirring constantly; cook and stir until thick and clear. Remove from heat; add 2 table-spoons lemon juice. Cool to room temperature. Pour over berries. Chill. If you like, garnish with whipped cream. Makes 12 servings.

CHOCOLATE CHEESE PIE

1 1/2 cups fine graham-cracker crumbs
1/2 cup melted butter or margarine
1 6-ounce package (1 cup) semisweet
    chocolate pieces
2 3-ounce packages cream cheese,
    softened
1/2 cup sugar
1 teaspoon vanilla
1/4 teaspoon salt
2 egg yolks
1 cup whipping cream, whipped
2 egg whites
1/4 cup sugar

Mix cracker crumbs and melted butter or mar-garine; press into a 9-inch pie plate. Chill.

Melt chocolate pieces over hot, *not boiling* water. Cool slightly. Blend cream cheese, 1/2 cup sugar, vanilla, and salt. Add yolks, one at a time, beating well after each. Stir in melted chocolate; chill till thick; beat smooth. Fold whipped cream into chocolate. Beat egg whites to soft peaks. Gradually add 1/4 cup sugar, beat-ing to stiff peaks; fold into chocolate. Pile into crust. Place in freezer till chilled well; remove 5 to 10 minutes before serving.

RASPBERRY RIBBON PIE

1 3-ounce package raspberry-flavored
    gelatin
1/4 cup granulated sugar
1 10-ounce package frozen red
    raspberries
1 tablespoon lemon juice
1 3-ounce package cream cheese,
    softened
1/3 cup sifted confectioners' sugar
1 teaspoon vanilla
Dash salt
1 cup heavy cream, whipped
1 9-inch baked pastry shell, cooled

Red layers: Dissolve gelatin and 1/4 cup sugar in 1 1/4 cups boiling water. Add berries and lemon juice; stir till berries thaw. Chill till partially set. *White layers:* Meanwhile blend cheese, con-fectioners' sugar, vanilla, and salt. Fold in a small amount of whipped cream, then fold in remainder. Spread *half* the cheese mixture over bottom of pastry shell. Cover with *half* the red gelatin mixture. Repeat; chill till set.

PINEAPPLE JEWEL SQUARES

1 cup fine graham-cracker crumbs
2 tablespoons sugar
1/4 cup butter or margarine, melted
1 8 3/4-ounce can (1 cup) crushed
    pineapple
1 3-ounce package orange-pineapple-
    flavored gelatin
1 3-ounce package cream cheese,
    softened
3 tablespoons sugar
1/2 teaspoon vanilla
1/4 teaspoon grated orange peel
1 cup dairy sour cream

Mix crumbs, 2 tablespoons sugar, and butter; press into bottom of 8x8x2-inch baking dish. Chill. Drain pineapple *well*, reserving 1/2 cup syrup. Dissolve gelatin in 1 1/4 cups boiling wa-ter. Add pineapple syrup; cool. Blend cheese with 3 tablespoons sugar, vanilla, and orange peel. Stir 1/2 *cup gelatin* into pineapple, set aside. Gradually blend remaining gelatin into cheese mixture; stir in sour cream. Pour into crust; chill till firm. Spoon pineapple mixture over cheese layer. Chill 4 to 6 hours. Serves 6 to 9.

FRESH FRUIT TARTS

2 slightly beaten egg yolks
2 cups milk
1 3-ounce package vanilla pudding
   mix (dry)
2 3-ounce packages cream cheese
2 egg whites
¼ cup sugar
8 baked tart shells, 3½ inches in
   diameter
Fresh or canned fruits

Combine beaten egg yolks and milk. Cook pudding mix according to package directions using the egg-milk mixture as the liquid. Remove from heat. Cut cream cheese in pieces and add to hot pudding; beat till cheese is melted. Let mixture cool about 10 minutes.

Beat egg whites to soft peaks; gradually add sugar beating to stiff peaks. Fold egg whites into pudding. Spoon into tart shells; chill. Just before serving, spoon sugared fresh strawberries, fresh blueberries, or canned peach halves over tarts. Makes 8 servings.

Fresh Fruit Tarts sport flavorful fruit atop a creamy custard filling. Colorful and elegant, they're a great idea for entertaining. As fresh fruits come in season, use their colors, flavors, and textures to spectacular advantage with this dessert idea. Or, use canned fruits any time.

CREAM CHEESE COOKIES

Cream together 1 cup butter or margarine, two 3-ounce packages cream cheese, softened, 1 cup sugar, ¼ teaspoon salt, and 1 teaspoon vanilla. Add 1 egg and 2 tablespoons milk; beat well. Add 2 cups sifted all-purpose flour and stir in ½ cup toasted flaked coconut.* Drop from teaspoon onto ungreased baking sheet. Top with California walnut halves, if desired. Bake in a slow oven (325°) for about 20 minutes. Remove to cooling rack. Makes 5 dozen.

*To toast coconut, spread on baking sheet; heat and stir in 350° oven till lightly browned.

CHEESE-STUFFED APPLES

**1 3-ounce package cream
  cheese, softened**
1⅓ ounces Camembert cheese
1 tablespoon white wine
4 medium apples

Beat cheeses and wine with electric mixer or rotary beater till smooth. Core apples; scoop out pulp leaving shell about ½-inch thick. Fill with cheese mixture; chill 2 to 3 hours. To serve, cut each in half or in wedges. Serve with assorted small crackers. Serves 8.

Fruit and cheese make dessert a special occasion. Here large wedges of deep orange Cheddar and delicate yellow Swiss stand high. Down front, a red-jacketed Edam has been sliced to show its golden interior. Crisp crackers and fresh juicy fruits complete this dessert.

BLUE CHEESE MELON DIP

Combine one 4-ounce package blue cheese, one 3-ounce package cream cheese, 2 tablespoons milk, and 2 tablespoons mayonnaise. Beat at low speed of electric mixer till light and fluffy. Makes about 1 cup.

FROZEN CRANBERRY ANGEL CAKE

1 loaf-style angel food cake
1 3-ounce package cream cheese, softened
¼ cup sugar
Dash salt
1 cup whipping cream, whipped
1 1-pound can (2 cups) whole cranberry sauce

Cut cake into ½-inch slices and line bottom of 8½x4½x2¾-inch loaf dish. Cream together cheese, sugar, and salt till fluffy. Fold in whipped cream. Stir cranberry sauce to break up; fold into cheese mixture.

Spoon ½ the cranberry mixture over cake slices. Place another layer of cake slices over mixture and top with remaining cranberry mixture. Freeze overnight. Serves 8.

PINEAPPLE CHEESE PARFAITS

Tastes like cheesecake in a parfait glass—

1 2¾-ounce package vanilla custard mix (no-bake type)
2 cups milk
. . .
2 3-ounce packages cream cheese, softened
½ teaspoon vanilla
1 1-pound 5-ounce can pineapple pie filling

In saucepan, prepare custard according to the package directions using the milk. Remove from heat. Gradually stir hot mixture into cheese; mix well. Stir in vanilla. Chill custard and pie filling till serving time. When ready to serve, spoon alternate layers of custard and pie filling into parfait glasses. Top with additional pie filling if desired. Serves 6 to 8.

Frosted Green Grapes add elegance to any cheese-fruit dessert tray. Combine slightly beaten egg white with a little water; brush over clusters of grapes, then sprinkle with granulated sugar. Place on a rack till sugar is dry.

ROQUEFORT DESSERT SPREAD

8 ounces (2 cups) Roquefort cheese
1 tablespoon sauterne
3 tablespoons diced almonds, toasted

With electric or rotary beater, whip together cheese and sauterne till light and fluffy. Stir in toasted almonds. Form mixture into a bar; chill. Slice and serve with fresh fruit.

SPICY PUMPKIN PIE

Cream cheese helps make this traditional favorite so smooth—

Beat together one 8-ounce package cream cheese, softened, ¾ cup brown sugar, 1 teaspoon cinnamon, 1 teaspoon nutmeg, ½ teaspoon ginger, and ½ teaspoon salt. Add 3 eggs, one at a time, beating well after each addition. Stir in 1 cup canned or mashed cooked pumpkin, 1 cup milk, and 1 teaspoon vanilla. Pour mixture into one unbaked 9-inch pastry shell.

Bake in a moderate oven (375°) for 45 to 50 minutes or till knife inserted halfway between center and edge comes out clean. Chill thoroughly before serving. If desired, garnish with whipped cream and sprinkle with nutmeg.

These cheeses are worth knowing. Try any of the selection pictured above with your favorite fruits, or in dips or spreads for delicious new dessert ideas.

1 Provolone (salami-style)
2 Longhorn
3 Midget Cheddar (sharp)
4 Gorgonzola
5 Parmesan
6 Edam
7 Cheddar (sharp)
8 Cheddar (soft)
9 Port du Salut
10 Provolone
11 Smoked Swiss
12 Cheddar (medium-sharp)
13 Swiss
14 Roquefort
15 Cheshire
16 Sapsago
17 Stilton
18 Gourmandise
19 Sharp Cheddar spread
20 Cheddar (sliced)
21 Pimiento cream-cheese dip
22 Bel Paese
23 Grape cheese
24 Bondost
25 Bondost with caraway seed
26 Christian IX (Danish spiced)
27 Herkimer (a Cheddar type)
28 Sage

CHEESE GUIDE TO GOOD DESSERT EATING

Cheese	How it looks and tastes	How to serve
Blue Gorgonzola *(gor-gun-zo'-luh)* Roquefort *(rok-for')* Stilton	Compact, creamy cheeses veined with blue or blue-green mold. Sometimes crumbly. Mild to sharp, salty flavor.	At room temperature with fresh apples and pears, crackers, or crusty French or Italian bread.
Brick	About brick size; texture ranging from soft to firm with many tiny round holes. Creamy yellow color; mild to moderately sharp flavor.	Especially good with fresh peaches, apricots, cherries, or melon. Or, string cubes on toothpicks with chunks of fresh apple and pear.
Brie *(bree)*	Soft-ripening, similar to Camembert, but slightly firmer. Creamy yellow with thin brown and white crust. Mild to pungent flavor; pronounced odor.	With fresh peaches or pears. Be sure to eat the crust. Good with a variety of dark, whole-grain breads.
Camembert *(kam'-em-bear)*	Creamy yellow inside with a thin gray-white crust. When ripe it softens to the consistency of thick cream. Full, rich, mildly pungent flavor.	One of the world's classic dessert cheeses. Leave at room temperature before serving for best eating quality—the consistency of thick cream is ideal. Team with fresh peaches, apples, and pears, or with fresh tart plums and cracked roasted walnuts. The crust is good eating, too.
Chantelle *(shahn-tell')*	Pale yellow interior with a red coat. Mellow flavor; semisoft texture.	Best with red or yellow apples.
Cheddar or American	Favorite all-round firm cheese. Flavor varies from mild to sharp. Color ranges from natural to yellow-orange; texture from firm to crumbly. May come in wedges, sticks, rectangular cuts called "blunts," slices, or cubes. Also available in process form.	Excellent with fruit pie, crisp crackers, fresh cherries or pears.
Cream	Soft buttery texture; very mild flavor; rich and smooth. Comes plain, whipped, or flavored with pineapple, dates and nuts, etc.	Thin with cream and serve with crackers and your favorite jellies. Also good with preserved kumquats, fresh apricots, grapes, peaches, and pears, sectioned oranges, and salted nuts.
Edam, Gouda *(ee'-dum, goo'-da)*	Round, red-coated; creamy yellow to yellow-orange inside; firm, smooth texture. Mild sweet nutlike flavor. "Baby Gouda" weighs less than a pound, Edam weighs 2 to 4 pounds.	Bright hub for dessert tray. Serve in wedges, or cut off top; hollow out center; dice and refill. Or, let each person scoop out his own. Best fruits are fresh grapes, peeled oranges.
Liederkranz *(lee'-dir-krahnz)*	Soft-ripening; robust flavor and odor resembling Limburger. Golden yellow color.	Spread on toast and crackers, rye and pumpernickel breads. Especially good with fresh apples, pears, and Tokay grapes.
Muenster *(mun'-stir)*	Similar to Brick cheese. Mild and mellow flavor; white creamy. Medium hard with tiny holes. Now made in the United States, but longer European curing time makes a sharper flavor.	Serve with fresh dark cherries and wedges of canteloupe or honeydew melon.
Process cheeses American Brick Gruyere *(gree-air')* Swiss Others	Smooth, creamy texture. Spreads easily at room temperature; sliced when chilled. Melts smoothly and quickly. Selected lots of fresh and aged natural cheeses are blended and pasteurized so that no further ripening takes place. May be flavored with bacon, pineapple, etc.	Serve at room temperature to spread on crusty French or Italian bread. Chill to cut in thin slices or cubes. Goes well with many fruits.
Swiss	Firm, pale yellow cheese, with large round holes. Mild, sweet, nutlike flavor. Comes in chunks or already sliced.	With fresh apricots, grapes, melon wedges, peaches, or sectioned oranges, and tangerines. Or, serve with dark breads and fruit juice.
Cheese Spreads	Glassed and packaged ready-to-spread blends; mild to very sharp. Plain or flavored with smoke, relish, olive, pineapple, garlic, or pepper. Like process cheese but with higher moisture and lower milk fat content. Added stabilizer prevents separation.	With crackers or your favorite bread. Good with most fruits.

CREAM CHEESE BROWNIES

Melt 2 ounces (2 squares) unsweetened chocolate and 3 tablespoons butter or margarine over low heat. Cool and set aside.

In small mixing bowl, cream together one 3-ounce package cream cheese and 2 tablespoons butter. Gradually add ¼ cup sugar; beat till fluffy. Add 1 egg, ½ teaspoon vanilla, and 1 tablespoon all-purpose flour; mix well.

In second bowl, beat 2 eggs till light; gradually add ¾ cup sugar; beat till thick and lemon colored. Add the melted, cooled chocolate and 1 teaspoon vanilla. Stir in ⅔ cup sifted all-purpose flour, ½ teaspoon baking powder, ¼ teaspoon salt, and ½ cup chopped California walnuts. Turn ¾ of the chocolate batter into a greased 9-inch square pan. Top with cream cheese batter. Spoon remaining chocolate batter over all; cut through to marble. Bake at 350° for 30 minutes or till done. Cool and cut into squares. Makes 16 to 20.

CREAM CHEESE FROSTING

**1 3-ounce package cream cheese,
  softened
1 tablespoon butter, softened
1 teaspoon vanilla
2 cups sifted confectioners' sugar
Milk**

Blend cheese, butter, and vanilla. Beat till light. Gradually add sugar, creaming well. Add enough milk to make mixture of spreading consistency. Frosts one 8- or 9-inch square cake.

CREAM CHEESE FREEZE

**2 3-ounce packages cream cheese,
  softened
⅔ cup sugar
2½ teaspoons vanilla
2 cups light cream**

Cream together the cheese, sugar, and vanilla. Slowly add the cream, mixing thoroughly. Freeze in refrigerator tray till firm; break in chunks and beat with electric mixer till smooth.* Return to tray; freeze firm. Makes 6 servings.

*Or freeze in refrigerator tray till partially frozen; beat smooth with rotary beater.

CHOCOLATE CLOUD SOUFFLE

**⅓ cup light cream
1 3-ounce package cream cheese
½ cup semisweet chocolate pieces
3 egg yolks
Dash salt
3 egg whites
3 tablespoons confectioners' sugar**

Blend cream and cream cheese over very *low* heat. Add chocolate pieces; heat and stir till melted. Cool. Beat egg yolks and salt till thick and lemon colored. Gradually blend into chocolate mixture. Beat egg whites till soft peaks form. Gradually add sugar, beating to stiff peaks; fold in chocolate mixture. Pour into *ungreased* 1-quart souffle dish or casserole. Bake in slow oven (300°) for 45 minutes or till knife inserted comes out clean. Serves 5 or 6.

CREAMY APPLE CHEESE BAKE

Crust: Combine 1 cup sifted all-purpose flour, 1 tablespoon sugar, and dash salt; finely cut in ¼ cup butter or margarine. Combine 1 slightly beaten egg yolk with 1 teaspoon water; blend into crumb mixture. Press on bottom and sides of 8x8x2-inch baking pan.

Filling: Drain one 1-pound 4-ounce can unsweetened sliced apples; add ⅓ cup sugar, 1 teaspoon lemon juice, and ¼ teaspoon *each* cinnamon and nutmeg. Turn into crust; bake at 425° for 10 minutes. Meanwhile, mix ½ cup sugar, 2 slightly beaten eggs, 4 ounces *whipped* cream cheese, and dash salt. Blend in ½ cup whipping cream; add 1 teaspoon vanilla. Pour over apples. Bake at 350° for 30 to 35 minutes or till set. Chill. Serves 8 or 9.

CREAM CHEESE SHERBET

Mix 1½ teaspoons unflavored gelatin with 1½ cups sugar; add one 7½-ounce can (1 cup) unsweetened pineapple juice. Heat and stir till gelatin and sugar dissolve. Remove from heat; add 1 cup orange juice and 3 tablespoons lemon juice. Cool. Blend one 8-ounce package cream cheese with ¼ teaspoon salt; gradually beat in juice mixture and ½ teaspoon almond extract. Whip 1 cup whipping cream; fold in. Pour into 2-quart refrigerator tray; freeze 6 to 8 hours.

A

American Cheese, 10, 87
Appetizer, 40-47
  Biscuits, Hibachi
    Cheese, 46
  Camembert, French-
    fried, 47
  Chili Cheese Log, 45
  Dip
    Anchovy-cheese, 43
    Bean-cheese, 44
    Blue Cheese, 42
    Blue Cheese,
      Creamy, 42
    Cheddar, 42
    Clam-cheese, 44
    Crab, Hot Cheese
      'n, 42
    Diet, Dip Away, 42
    Fluff, Cheese, 43
    Fruit, Hot Cheese
      Dip with, 45
    Jiffy, 43
    Lobster Dip
      Elegante, 45
    Low-calorie, 42
  Dried Beef Log, 42
  Edam, Festive, 43
  Mousse, Appetizer
    Cheese, 44
  Mushrooms, Cheese-
    stuffed, 46
  Olive Bites, 46
  Olive Canapes,
    Broiled, 47
  Olive-cheese Ball, 45
  Parmesan Shoe-
    strings, 46
  Pinwheels, Toasty
    Cheese, 47
  Pizzas, Piccolo, 46
  Sausage Bites, 46
  Shrimp-cheese
    Fondue, 45
  Shrimp Cheese
    Turnovers, 47
  Spreads, 43
  Sticks, Cheese, 46
  Swiss-frank
    Roll-ups, 47
  Swiss Sandwich
    Puffs, 47
  Tuna Pate, 45

B-C

Bel Paese Cheese, 7, 86
Blarney Cheese, 9
Blue Cheese, 7, 87
  Appetizer Cheese
    Mousse, 44
  Broccoli Casserole, 69
  Cauliflower Cheese
    Toss, 65
  Clam-cheese Dip, 44

Dips, 42
Dressing, Creamy, 66
Fondue, Rosy
  Cheese, 30
Melon Dip, 85
Mold, Frosted
  Cheese, 62
Mushrooms, Blue-
  cheesed, 69
Olive-cheese Ball, 45
Sauce, Zippy, 74
Spread, Three
  Cheese, 43
Topper, 56
Waldorf Salad, 63
Bondost Cheese, 86
Bread, 48-52
  Biscuits, 46, 52
  Blintzes, Israeli
    Cheese, 52
  Bowl, Toasted
    Cheese, 39
  Brunch Bites, 52
  Crescents, Cheese, 50
  Easy Cheese, 52
  Loaves, 50, 52
  Muffins, Cheddar
    Bran, 50
  Olive Pizza, 51
  Puris, 51
  Rolls, Airy Cheese, 50
  -soup Bread,
    Cheese, 51
  Spoon Bread,
    Bacon, 51
  Sticks, Cheese, 51
Brick Cheese, 7, 87
Brie Cheese, 7, 87
Camembert
  Cheese, 6, 87
Casseroles, *see Main
  Dishes*
Chantelle Cheese, 87
Cheddar Cheese, 9
  86, 87
Cheese Spreads, 10,
  86, 87
Cheshire Cheese, 86
Christian IX Cheese, 86
Club Cheese, 6
Cooking and Serving, 11
Cottage Cheese, 6
Cream Cheese, 6, 86, 87

D

Desserts, 76, 88
  Apple Cheese Bake,
    Creamy, 88
  Apples, Cheese-
    stuffed, 84
  Brownies, Cream

    Cheese, 88
  Cake, Frozen Cran-
    berry Angel, 85
  Cheese Guide, 86, 87
  Cheesecake
    Angel, 78
    Cafe Au Lait, 78
    Cherry Cheese-
      cakes, Petite, 79
    Honey-raisin, 79
    Marble, 78
    Pudding 'n Pine-
      apple Cake, 79
    Strawberry-
      Glazed, 80
    Supreme, 80
    Surprise, 79
  Cookies, Cream
    Cheese, 84
  Dip, Blue Cheese
    Melon, 85
  Freeze, Cream
    Cheese, 88
  Frosting, Cream
    Cheese, 88
  Pie, Chocolate
    Cheese, 82
  Pie, Raspberry
    Ribbon, 82
  Pie, Spicy
    Pumpkin, 85
  Pineapple Cheese
    Parfaits, 85
  Pineapple Jewel
    Squares, 82
  Sherbet, Cream
    Cheese, 88
  Souffle, Chocolate
    Cloud, 88
  Spread, Roquefort, 85
  Tart, French Straw-
    berry, 82
  Tarts, Fresh Fruit, 83
Double Gloucester
  Cheese, 9

E-F-G

Edam, 9, 86, 87
Fish, *see Main Dishes*
Fondue, *see Main Dishes*
Fontina Cheese, 9
Gjetost Cheese, 9
Gorgonzola, 86, 87
Gouda Cheese, 9, 87
Gourmandise
  Cheese, 6, 86
Grape Cheese, 86
Grapes, Frosted, 85
Gruyere, 8, 87

H-L-M

Herkimer Cheese, 86
Liederkranz
  Cheese, 6, 87

Limburger Cheese, 7
Longhorn Cheese, 86
Main Dishes, 12-39
  Bacon and Eggs,
    Scalloped, 16
  Blintze, Country, 23
  Casserole
    Chicken Bake,
      Three Cheese, 37
    Chicken
      Macaroni, 20
    Chicken-rice
      Divan, 37
    Corned Beef Supper
      Special, 15
    Franks Floren-
      tine, 14
    Hamburger-cheese
      Delight, 14
    Macaroni and
      Cheese Bake,
      Creamy, 20
    Macaroni And
      Cheese,
      Classic, 18
    Macaroni and Sau-
      sage Bake, 19
    Meat 'n Macaroni
      Supper, 19
    Mexi-chili, 15
    Noodle Bake, Hun-
      garian, 14
    Ravioli, Inside-
      out, 21
    Salmon
      Macaroni, 19
    Sea Food, 38
    Shrimp Bake, 38
    Skillet Supper,
      Family, 34
    Swiss Luncheon
      Special, 15
    Tuna Bake, Com-
      pany, 21
    Tuna-spaghetti
      Bake, 19
    Turkey,
      Cheddar, 37
  Cheese-rice
    Squares, 15
  Chiles Rellenos con
    Queso, 27
  Crab 'n Mushrooms
    Mornay, 38
  Eggs, Cheesed
    Scrambled, 23
  Eggs, Shrimp-
    curried, 25
  Enchiladas,
    Cheese, 27
  Fondue
    Baked Cheese, 16
    Blender Cheese, 30
    Classic Cheese, 30
    Lore, 30
    Rosy Cheese, 30

Ham Salad,
  Skillet, 65
Lasagne, Baked, 21
Lasagne, Lazy-
  day, 21
Meat
  Burgers, Pin-
    wheel, 35
  Cheese Round
    Steak, 33
  Loaf, Cheese-
    filled, 35
  Loaf—Italian
    Style, 35
  Pork Chops,
    Cheese-
    stuffed, 33
  Rib Roast, Stuffed
    Rolled, 35
  Saucy Meatball
    Supper, 34
  Steak Rolls,
    Minute, 35
  Veal Foldovers,
    Swiss, 33
  Veal Parmigiano, 33
Noodles Romano, 14
Omelet, Cheese
  French, 23
Omelet, Parmesan, 23
Oyster Pudding, 38
Peppers, Old-time
  Stuffed, 67
Pie, Swiss, 22
Poultry
  Chicken Bake,
    Three Cheese, 37
  Chicken Macaroni
    Casserole, 20
  Chicken-rice
    Divan, 37
  Chicken Washing-
    ton, Rolled, 37
  Turkey Casserole,
    Cheddar, 37
Quiche Lorraine, 23
Rabbit
  Cheese, 32
  Classic Cheese, 32
  Double Cheese, 32
  Golden Velvet, 32
  Mexican, 32
  Quick Cheese, 32
Souffle
  Cheese, 25
  Collar, 24
  Easy Cheese, 25
  Swiss Rice, 16
  Tapioca Cheese, 25
Strata, Classic
  Cheese, 16
Strata, Company, 17
Monterey Jack
  Cheese, 8
Mozzarella Cheese, 8
Muenster Cheese, 8, 87

N-P-R

Neufchatel Cheese, 7
Parmesan Cheese, 10, 86
Pies, see Desserts
Pizza
  Bread, Olive, 51
  Crust, Homemade, 29
  Crust, Jiffy, 29
  Mushroom, 29
  Pepperoni, 29
  Piccolo Pizzas, 46
  Pronto, 55
  Sausage, 29
Port du Salut
  Cheese, 8, 86
Poultry, see Main
  Dishes
Process Cheeses, 10, 87
Provolone Cheese,
  9, 86
Rabbit, Rarebit, see
  Main Dishes
Ricotta Cheese, 7
Riksost Cheese, 10
Romano Cheese, 10
Roquefort Cheese,
  8, 86, 87
Salad Toss, 64
Spread, Roquefort
  Dessert, 85

S

Sage Cheese, 86
Salad, 60-66
  Avocado Fruit
    Squares, 63
  Carrot Relish
    Cups, 63
  Cauliflower Cheese
    Toss, 65
  Chef's Salad Bowl, 64
  Cocktail Slices,
    Frozen, 63
  -cucumber Ring,
    Cool-as-a, 63
  Ham Salad Mold, 64
  Ham Salad, Skillet, 65
  Macaroni-and-
    cheese, 65
  Mold, Frosted
    Cheese, 62
  Orange Molds,
    Frozen, 62
  Peach Melba Mold, 62
  Plum Squares,
    Greengage, 63
  Potato, Cottage, 65
  Strawberry Cream
    Freeze, 62
  Tomato Filling,
    Stuffed, 64
  Toss, 64
  Tuna Ring,
    Creamy, 65

Waldorf, Blue
  Cheese, 63
Salad Dressing
  Blue Cheese Dressing,
    Creamy, 66
  Low Calorie Horse-
    radish Dressing, 66
  Orange Dressing,
    Fluffy, 66
Sandwiches, 53-59
  Hearty
    Antipasto, 57
    Beanwich,
      Boston, 53
    -beef, Double, 57
    Cheeseburger
      Towers, 56
    Chicken Cheese
      Puff, 55
    Crab, Toasted, 53
    Denvers, Dad's, 55
    Grilled Cheese
      Italiano, 53
    Ham and Cheese,
      Jiffy, 53
    Ham Buns, Hot, 55
    Ham 'n Cheese
      French Toast, 53
    Loaf, Ten-in-one
      Sandwich, 56
    Marshall Field's
      Special, 57
    Meat-cheese Open
      Facers, 55
    Pizza, Inside-
      out, 53
    Pizza Pronto, 55
    Reuben, Grilled, 53
    Swiss, Toasted, 53
    Torpedoes, 57
  Party
    Chutney-cheese
      Rounds, 58
    Date-roll, 58
    Filling, Party
      Sandwich, 58
    Jigsaw, 59
    Loaf, Frosted Rib-
      bon, 58
    Olive Canapes,
      Broiled, 47
    Pinwheels, Deviled
      Ham, 59
    Pinwheels, Toasty
      Cheese, 47
    Pinwheels, Water
      Cress, 59
    Shrimp
      Triangles, 58
    Swiss Sandwich
      Puffs, 47
Sapsago Cheese, 10, 86
Sauce, 74-75
  Blue Cheese,
    Zippy, 74
  Caraway Cheese, 75

Cheddar Cheese, 23
Cheddar Cheese
  Sauces, 74
Cheese, Chef's, 75
Chive, 75
Egg, Cheesy, 75
Hollandaise,
  Mock, 75
Horseradish, 75
Mornay, 74
Parmesan,
  Imperial, 74
Shrimp, 25
Shrimp Almond, 75
Shrimp Cheese, 75
Swiss-Cheddar, 74
Swiss Cheese, 74
Scamorze Cheese, 8
Serving, Cooking and, 11
Souffles, see Main
  Dishes
Soup, 70-73
  Asparagus,
    Cheesy, 73
  Canadian Cheese, 72
  Cheese, Golden, 73
  Chowder, Chicken-
    cheese, 73
  Chowder, Pacific, 73
  Onion and Cheese, 72
  Potato, Alpine, 73
  Vichyssoise,
    Quick, 73
Stilton Cheese, 86, 87
Storage of Cheese, 11
Swiss Cheese, 10, 86, 87
Tilsit Cheese, 8

V-W

Vegetables, 67-69
  Artichoke Velvet, 68
  Broccoli Casserole, 69
  Carrots Au
    Gratin, 68
  Cauliflower,
    Company, 68
  Corn, Creamy, 68
  Eggplant, Cheese
    Broiled, 69
  Green Bean-cheese
    Bake, 69
  Limas, De Luxe, 69
  Mushrooms, Blue-
    cheesed, 69
  Onions, Cheese
    Stuffed, 69
  Peppers, Old-time
    Stuffed, 67
  Potatoes Au
    Gratin, 67
  Tomato Casserole, 67
  Vegetable Bake
    Company, 68
  Zucchini Boats, 67
Wine Information, 11

Additional recipes

Pages of this final section are for adding recipes from future issues of Better Homes and Gardens magazine and other favorite cheese recipes.